ONE OVER PAR

'Why, I asked my father, was it necessary to have so many priests in attendance on one golfer?' (*Miles Kington, page* 127)

ONE OVER PAR

A Connoisseur's Golfing Anthology

Edited by Peter Alliss and
Mike Seabrook

Illustrations by Bill Tidy

H. F. & G. WITHERBY LTD

This anthology first published in Great Britain 1992 by
H.F. & G. Witherby Ltd
14 Henrietta Street, London WC2E 8QJ

ISBN 0 85493 214 3

Photoset by Rowland Phototypesetting Ltd
Printed in Great Britain by St Edmundsbury Press Ltd
Bury St Edmunds, Suffolk

CONTENTS

INTRODUCTION

Mike Seabrook

If games were originally devised as pleasures, as escapes from work, as fun, these days one would be forgiven for forgetting the fact. Football is often synonymous with behaviour reminiscent of the *Sturmabteilung*. Pat Cash damned women's tennis as vacuum-packed sterility, only to spoil a nice point by forgetting to add that the only thing worse than the metronomic tedium of women's tennis is the endless self-recycling brainlessness of serve and volley to which men's tennis is diminished. The world of athletics periodically tears itself apart from within over the consumption of interesting chemicals in the cause of winning – attitudes to which have successfully reduced the Olympic Games to a cross between institutionalised shamateurism and nationalism in its most mindless excesses of flag-wagging, anthem-blaring awfulness. Even cricket, which has retained more of its soul than most games, has been riven at its highest level by everything from apartheid to bouncers, from time-wasting to public finger-wagging contests and exchanges of four-letter words between captains and umpires, from throwing to Neronian orgies of booze, sex and dope.

But behind all the lurid headlines about the sleazier side of sport, one game has gone quietly and unobtrusively on, being played by more people than almost any other ball game, almost free from all the unpleasantness and controversy, simply providing vast amounts of pleasure. That game is golf.

It is a game of strong passions. In its devotees it tends to inspire unshakeable, not to say fanatical, loyalty; its detractors tend to be equally unequivocal in their loathing for it. One has only to look at the best-known quotes about the game to see this. Everyone knows Mark Twain's snide but happily expressed gibe that a round of golf is 'a good walk spoiled'; Bernard Shaw spoke of 'cricketers, to whom old age brings not wisdom but golf' (he said it, of course, as he said most of his best *bons mots*, in order to demonstrate his own superiority to the benighted lesser mortals who chose to like the despised pastimes, and as usual succeeded only in demonstrating what an insufferable ass he could be when he was feeling superior to people; but it's a good one-liner, all the same).

Even the delectable quotes that aren't actually anti-golf tend to have a faintly defensive air about them. Thus Stephen Leacock: 'Golf may be played on a Sunday, not being a game within the view of the law, but being a form of moral effort.' Or Eric Morecambe: 'My wife says if I don't give up golf she'll leave me.' 'That's terrible,' replies Ernie Wise. 'I know,' says Eric, 'I'm really going to miss her.'

Of course, quotations are the opium of the essayist. And there are so many good ones about golf that one is tempted to dally with them all day, forgetting mundane matters like actually writing one's introduction. Of course such temptations must be resisted stoutly; but not before one last one is brought into the light, like a particularly cherished float, or pipe, or a little cup won at golf when one was a lad. My choice for the positively last quote of this introduction is from P. G. Wodehouse, and I choose it because it says so much about bad golfers – which is to say, of course, most golfers. 'The least thing upsets him on the links,' he said. 'He misses short putts because of the uproar of the butterflies in the adjoining meadows.'

All this helps to demonstrate: there aren't many mere golfers. Few people are neutral about the game. But for anyone with any feelings at all about it, pro or amateur, pro or anti, this book is the perfect bedside or fireside companion.

Unlike some games, notably cricket, golf has not inspired a particularly distinguished literature. This book helps to put that right. Here are twenty-odd writers, including some of the greatest and most famous in the world today, talking about golf. Most try to tell us what it is that makes them love the game. A few, for balance, try to explain why they *don't*. The one thing they have in common is that their writing is luminous and fascinating: they all illuminate, in very different ways, some way in which the game appeals, appals, compels or repels.

For example, four of the finest American novelists of the age divide fifty-fifty pro and anti. John Updike contributes an essay of crystalline beauty, attempting a definition of the game in prose of wit, elegance and geniality. His partner for the 'pros', Joseph Wambaugh, describes a hilarious match when two ordinary – and ordinarily skint – Los Angeles cops get to play at an impossibly exclusive rich-man's playground. No one who is even marginally a member of a species that laughs will be proof against the results.

Ranged against them for the 'antis', Richard Condon turns his versatile talents to a speculation that his equally versatile father may have given him a complex for life, as the cod-psychologist's term once had it, against the game; he is paired for the occasion by the master of the tough-talk law thriller, George V. Higgins, a lawyer himself, who gives us a witty account of how he took on golf and lost.

Playing for England, one of our foremost novelists and belletrists, Simon Raven, tells of appalling happenings on a golf course in his home county of Kent. His memorable story culminates in a development as sudden and as utterly unexpected as being struck by lightning.

Lightning finds its way into Lord Donald Soper's contribution. In a remarkable essay, unlike anything else in this collection, he seeks parallels between the game that is his private passion and the vocation to which he has very publicly devoted his life. To go with our eminent divine we have an eminent jurist, Sir (formerly Mr Justice) Michael Davies, recently retired from the High Court, where he represented his era in the long tradition of judicial wit. Here he describes one of the most unusual cases in which he was ever briefed in his career at the bar.

Our pages are thickly dotted with writers from the widely scattered assortment of postal addresses that one may still, perhaps, call 'Fleet Street'. In a rich variety of styles they explode the notion that writing for newspapers and writing fine prose are mutually exclusive. Lord Deedes – better, and affectionately, known as Bill of that ilk – takes us on a genial tour of his private picture gallery of golfing reveries and memories. Martin Johnson, the funniest sports reporter in British journalism, tells of hazards, pitfalls and disasters of the most eclectic and multi-national kind encountered in pursuit of his obsession with the game. Chris Plumridge writes in his greatly admired lyrical style about the appeal of the game that he has loved for a lifetime, played – exceptionally well, with a handicap of a mere three – for forty years and written about for twenty-five.

Miles Kington, of whom no more needs to be said than that he is the Beachcomber *de nos jours*, and Donald Trelford, a surprising combination to find in stuffy old England, of high-intellectual editor of heavyweight Sunday Paper and keen golf, cricket and snooker fancier, both recall their own golfing careers with zest. John Ebdon, who claims to be on the anti-golf minority among the contributors, tells of an amusing encounter with the kind of coarse golfer we've all met once at least. Brian Glanville contributes a short story on the taboo subject of anti-semitism on the part of certain golfing establishments, and finally among the Fleet Street contingent, Edward Pearce gives us a characteristic piece of controlled ferocity about what he sees as being wrong with the game.

Two operatic singers who live exactly one planet's diameter apart give us stories from their own lives: Dame Joan Hammond tells of her days as a champion golfer in the Australian sun. Ian Wallace remembers an ill-assorted match in Scotland, featuring himself at sixteen, his father and an eccentric aunt, the guest of honour, the Right Honourable Ramsay MacDonald, the Prime Minister, and Hamish, his caddy for the day: a can or two short of a sixpack, and the cause of a certain amount of anguish for the young Wallace. And from the world of the theatre without music, Jeremy Kemp tells of how, also in Scotland, he met one of the legends of the game and then went on to beat the Open Champion of the day.

The world of whimsical humour brings us Frank Muir, who tells us everything there is to know about golf, demolishing the game's pretensions and ending with a pun for which he should not be forgiven lightly. It brings also our genial illustrator, Bill Tidy, who as well as gracing our pages with his customary off-beat perceptions of the human race, solves the mystery of why there are no Russian golfers – and describes what happened when he found one.

The line-up is completed by the editors themselves. Peter Alliss was certainly born with a golf club in his hands, undoubtedly held in the correct grip, played the impossible game at the highest level and, if any man does, deserves the title of Britain's Mr Golf. Known all over the golfing world as a commentator of exemplary urbanity, he carries out a survey of the great golfers of the last half a lifetime, knowledgeable, affable, and instinct with a profound affection for the game. I, for my part, know one end of a golf club from another – and for the practical purposes of the game could hold it by either end for all the difference it would make to my game. Having scored a hole in one at the age of thirteen on a putting green I sagely retired at the zenith of my golfing career, and now enjoy my golf from the armchair, deriving particular pleasure from seeing some of the world's highest-paid sportsmen being manoeuvred into ridiculous and impossible positions by their chosen and beloved game. I had, however, the unique privilege of getting a personal world premiere of each of the other twenty-one pieces of fine, mostly brand-new writing that make up this collection, and that was more than compensation enough.

NOTE: Wherever possible, we were eager to commission brand-new pieces of writing from our contributors for this anthology. In a few cases, however, an author felt that he was unlikely to surpass something already written, or had written himself out on the subject of golf. In these few cases, where we were particularly keen that the writer in question should be represented, we bent our rule slightly to accommodate them. This applies to only three of our twenty-two writers, however, the remaining nineteen being completely new pieces. The fact of a piece having been seen before is stated where necessary.

GOLF IN THE DESERT

Joseph Wambaugh

This piece is taken from Joseph Wambaugh's novel, The
Secrets of Harry Bright. *Two Los Angeles detectives,
Sidney Blackpool and Otto Stringer, have been given an
off-duty investigation by Victor Watson, a millionaire.
Along with a large financial inducement, Watson has
played on the detectives' liking for golf by offering them
the chance to play on courses that they could otherwise
only have dreamed of playing. For non-American
readers' benefit, Presidents William McKinley and
Andrew Jackson are depicted on the US$500 and $20
bills respectively.*

The clubhouse at Tamarisk was brand-new, but the golf course
was old. Along with Thunderbird Country Club, it was the oldest
posh club in the desert. The detectives weren't certain what to do,
but started lugging their own clubs until a kid saw them and took
their golf bags, directing them to the locker room where they
changed shoes.

The new clubhouse was perfect for the desert: lots of glass
and space, decorated in desert pastels. There was a membership
roster on the wall inside the lobby. Otto saw Gregory Peck's
name and began getting panicky. He half expected to run into
Yoko Ono.

Although he'd played an occasional game of golf over the years,
Otto had never really gotten interested in the game until he started
working with Sidney Blackpool, a pretty good golfer. In their
months together, Sidney Blackpool had managed to get them some

play at a few of the second-line private clubs in Los Angeles County, which were goat tracks compared to the manicured perfection of the desert country clubs.

'Oh, my God, Sidney!' Otto said when they were standing with the club pro looking at the eighteenth green. 'I never seen anything like this. It's . . . it's . . . I used to date a girl with a pussy like that!'

'Green?' said the club pro.

'Velvet,' Otto said. 'It looks like velvet around that pin. And look at the fairways, not a blemish. Do you use Clearasil on them, or what?'

'Have fun, fellas,' the pro said. 'You'll make a threesome with Mister Rosenkrantz. He's on the first tee warming up.'

'Thanks much,' Sidney Blackpool said, needing to take Otto's elbow to get him away from the eighteenth green. The boy already had their clubs loaded on an electric golf cart and was wiping down their woods.

'Do we tip the kid or what?' Otto whispered.

'After we're through,' Sidney Blackpool said.

'Do we pay green fees or what? Is ten grand *enough* for green fees?'

'Relax. Victor Watson took care a everything,' Sidney Blackpool said. 'Imagine what it'd be like working for a guy like him.'

'Imagine what it'd be like living in a place like *this*, Sidney. I *gotta* find me a rich woman in this town!'

The man waiting on the first tee was about sixty-five years old and fatter than Otto Stringer, but stood only about five feet six. He wore a floppy golf cap that came to the top of his ears and plastic-rimmed glasses that kept slipping down his nose. He smoked a cigar that was bigger than a twelve-ounce sap.

'You must be Mister Guildenstern,' Otto said, sticking out his hand.

'I'm the other one,' the man said. 'Rosenkrantz with a *K*. Glad to know you boys.'

'He's Sidney Blackpool and I'm Otto Stringer. Thanks for letting us play.'

'Glad to do a favor for friends a Victor Watson,' he said. 'Call me Archie. What's your handicap?'

'He's about a twelve,' Otto said. 'Me, I'm a beginner. Thirty handicap oughtta do it.'

'Last guy told me that beat me like a whorehouse rug,' Archie Rosenkrantz said. 'So I give you fifteen strokes. Sidney, you give me three. How about we play for twenty bucks four ways. Front, back, automatic press on the back and totals.'

'Sounds okay,' Sidney Blackpool said. 'You go ahead and show us the way, Archie.'

While Archie Rosenkrantz was getting himself ready on the first tee, Otto felt the panic bubbling. He whispered to his partner, 'Did you trade President McKinley for a whole *bunch* a Andrew Jacksons? We never played for more than two bucks at Griffith Park!'

'We got money, don't worry,' his partner whispered back.

Just then, a mixed foursome drove up in two custom golf carts and parked at the tee. One golf cart was Chinese red, built to resemble a baby Rolls-Royce. The man driving was older than George Burns. The girl in Ultrasuede was younger than Brooke Shields. Otto felt eight eyes on him. Disapproving eyes, he figured. He was sure they knew he was a Griffith Park hacker.

Then Otto heard a sound that reminded him of the Samoan's hand colliding with the back of his skull. Fat old guy, my ass! The freaking ball rocketed out there 220 yards. Dead *straight*.

'Can we just pay you now and get it over with?' Sidney Blackpool asked, as he stepped up and stuck a tee in the ground.

'Lucky shot,' Archie said, puffing on the Havana.

Otto kept glancing behind him at the clubhouse. He just knew there must be fifty people looking out through the tinted glass. He held his breath for twenty seconds and blew it out. He flexed his fists, forearms and biceps, then relaxed them. When he'd whiff at Griffith Park to the delight of some plumber, it was no big deal. But in *this* place?

Sidney Blackpool smacked it as hard as Archie Rosenkrantz, and being younger and more limber, he got an extra fifteen yards out of it. The ball faded but settled on the right side of the fairway.

'You ain't so bad yourself, kid,' Archie said, chewing the cigar to bits. 'I ain't gonna get fat on you boys, I can see.'

Otto was starting to feel all wrong. His lime-green doubleknits suddenly bit at his crotch. His argyle sweater chafed his armpits. His golf shoes seemed to be rubbing blisters on his ankles though he hadn't walked twenty feet. Even his goddamn Ben Hogan cap was too tight. He was a wreck.

Otto took a practice swing and sent a thirteen-inch slab of Tamarisk flying twenty yards. He ran off the tee and retrieved the turf while Archie Rosenkrantz puffed on the Havana and said, 'There's an eighty-year-old member here wears a toup looks just like that divot, 'cept his is orange. Don't be scared, kid. Just kick back and L.T.F.F.'

'What's L.T.F.F.?' Otto asked, feeling his jaws going tight.

'Let the fucker fly,' Archie said.

But suddenly Otto's golf gremlin showed up! His fear gremlin looked like Renfield, that giggling little fly-eater in the old movie who leads you to your room in the west tower and tells you to ignore that flapping outside the window because it's just some old drag queen from Bucharest and if you give him a peek at your bare bum and some warm milk with a Tollhouse cookie he'll flutter on home. Sure.

'Let the fucker fly,' said Otto bravely.

'Heh heh heh,' said Renfield, crunching on a blood-bloated horsefly as big as a pistachio.

Otto let the fucker fly all right.

'That wouldn't be a bad distance,' Archie said, 'if that was the ball instead a the club.'

'I can't understand it!' Otto cried, looking over his shoulder at the mixed foursome who were getting a real bang out of the gifted athlete on the first tee.

Sidney Blackpool trotted out to retrieve the graphite driver and Archie said, 'Tell you what, son, let's call off the bets. This frigging game's got enough stress built in. Let's just go out and have some fun, enjoy the day, have a laugh or two and a drink later.'

'Okay by me,' Sidney Blackpool said, handing Otto his driver.

Otto told himself it'd be easy now. The pressure was off. Except that the women in the mixed foursome were whispering, and Otto's ears were the colour of the pink argyles on his tummy. Still, he forced himself to move that club low and slow. He took it back slower than Don January ever thought of doing. He was feeling loose and dreamy. He was sooo slow. He was sooo relaxed he just might fall asleep. Except that just as he got that club past horizontal, Renfield said, 'There's nothing to fear but fear itself. Heh heh heh heeeee!' Otto knew that hovering rodent outside the window *only* had the face of Bela fucking Lugosi!

Otto gave it a Reggie Jackson fast-ball swing. With the same result. He whiffed that baby so bad he torqued like a licorice twist and found his head looking straight behind him like a cockatoo. Right at the two women in the mixed foursome who were beaming like two stews on Aloha Airlines: 'Welcome to paradise, stranger!'

'So I lied,' Renfield said, his teeth full of flies.

Archie Rosenkrantz almost lost his cigar. 'Did I hear a growl?' he cried. 'Lon Chaney needed a full moon to lunge like that!'

'Let's forget the first tee,' Sidney Blackpool suggested. 'Otto'll settle down after we get out on the fairway.'

'Palm Springs ain't heard a bigger swish since Liberace came to town,' Archie said. 'Okay, let's move along. My varicose veins're break dancing.'

The first hole was a five-par, 483 yarder, which shouldn't have caused too many problems. Otto was allowed to place his ball 200 yards out, near the drives hit by his playing partners.

'Now, Otto,' Archie said. 'There ain't nobody watching you so just step up there and look around at the mountains and smell the flowers and think how lucky you are that God gave you this happy day. Just say this to yourself: Aw, fuck it! And if I can't fuck it, I'll cover it with chocolate like old Mary See!'

So Otto stepped up and addressed the ball, letting his arms and forearms and wrists and hips and legs go limp and thought, 'Fuck it or cover it with chocolate.' And he let er fly and heard a dull thunk.

'Where is it?' Otto asked, shielding his eyes from the sun. 'Did it come down yet?'

'Worm burner,' Sidney Blackpool said.

'Bug fucker,' Archie Rosenkrantz said. 'Not *real* bad though. You got maybe thirty yards.'

Archie laid into his shot with a three wood, and his short back-swing put it out there nearly 200 yards, leaving him a pitch to the green.

Sidney Blackpool hit his three wood farther but drew it too much and faced a tricky wedge shot.

Otto incinerated a battalion of worms and ravished a bunch of bugs before finishing the first hole. In fact, when he landed in the trap on the right side he had his worst moment. Sidney Blackpool and Archie Rosenkrantz both dumped their third shots into the trap on the left, making it three on the beach and everyone moaning.

Archie blasted his out nicely and it landed twenty-five feet past the pin while Otto stared at his own sand shot and felt his sphincter tighten.

'Nice out,' Otto said enviously.

Sidney Blackpool took a bit too much sand but got away with it and his ball landed on the green and took a good roll thirty feet short of the flag. Otto felt his sphincter get tighter.

'Nice out,' Otto said enviously.

Then it was his turn. Otto lowered that wedge until it just brushed the sand two inches behind that ball, and tried to ignore Renfield's demented cackle.

Otto made a solemn vow that he was going to let his entire body relax no matter what happened to the sand shot. And he succeeded. He let his entire body go utterly limp and loose. He was sooo slow. He was sooo loose that he farted.

'Nice out,' Archie Rosenkrantz said enviously.

All in all it wasn't a bad day. Otto started to get better after checking in with a slick seven on the four-par third hole.

After five holes Archie said, 'You got a full house, Otto: three nines and a pair a sevens.'

On the four-par number six, Otto actually sank his second putt for a bogey five. 'Fever!' Otto cried. 'Gimme a fever!'

'Five for Otto!' Archie said, writing his score on the steering wheel card holder. 'Now you're cooking, kiddo. You finally stopped looking like Gary Gilmore with a target pinned to his shirt.'

'I got a five,' Sidney Blackpool said.

'No blood,' Archie said. 'We tied on that one.'

'Otto, let's give you the honours.'

Otto Stringer was so stoked from his bogey that he let it fly, but got under the ball. It was a 200-yard tee shot. Straight up.

'Where'd it go? Where'd it go?' Otto wanted to know.

'Fair catch,' Archie Rosenkrantz said. 'No run back on that one.'

By the time they reached the sixteenth hole, Otto had transferred his clubs on to the golf cart driven by Archie Rosenkrantz. Archie had told them that he was the father of two psychiatrists and Otto figured he might be able to help his golf swing.

'See, Archie,' Otto said while they waited for a twosome who were lost in the eucalyptus trees. 'It's like I got no muscle memory. My golfing muscles're forty years old and they already got Alzheimer's disease.'

'It's the muscle in your head's the problem, Otto,' Archie said, lighting a fresh Havana since the old one looked like spinach. 'The toughest six inches in golf is between your ears, right? You take it too serious. I wanna see you loosey goosey up there on the eighteenth tee.'

'It could be my basal ganglia,' Otto offered. 'That's what allows you to ride a bike or swing a golf club without thinking.'

'L.T.F.F., Otto.'

The eighteenth was a beauty, 522 yards looking right at the new clubhouse, which was framed by San Jacinto Peak. The fairway was lined by trees: pepper, palm, pine, willow, olive and rows of eucalyptus. There was flowing oleander on the right, which made Otto tense. He didn't want to fade into the bushes.

'I slice into that stuff I may as well eat some and die,' Otto said to Archie.

'Now you ain't gonna slice, Otto,' Archie said soothingly. 'Straight back and through and easy.'

'And look at all that eucalyptus!' Otto said. 'Enough to feed every koala in Australia.'

'Now stop those negative thoughts, Otto,' Archie said, while Sidney Blackpool sat with his feet up on the empty seat in his golf cart, looking at a smear of sunlight on the side of the mountain.

'I sure wanna finish strong,' Otto said. 'But what if I duck hook like I did on number three? Sometimes I lose my banana slice and find a duck hook. I might duck hook right into that house on the left.'

Then Otto looked curiously at the fenced property beside the fairway. It was totally enclosed, with security lights all the way round. There was a sign on one gate that said: 'Never mind the dog. Beware of the owner.' There was an American flag flying to indicate that the owner was in residence.

Otto made the mistake of asking who lived there, after which his golf swing was doomed.

Sidney Blackpool was startled when Otto ran to his golf cart and shook him by the shoulder.

'Sidney!' Otto cried. 'Do you know who lives over there? Him! Him!'

'Whom? Whom?'

'The Boss!'

'Bruce Springsteen?'

'The boss of bosses!'

'Don Corleone?'

'The Chairman of the Board!'

'Armand Hammer or Lee Iacocca?'

'Don't be stupid. Ol' blue eyes himself!'

'Yeah?' Even Sidney Blackpool looked a bit impressed. 'I thought his house might be a little more grand.'

'Whaddaya want? The guy's from Hoboken.'

'Well, he's not gonna ask us in,' Sidney Blackpool said. 'So let's tee 'er up and get to the nineteenth where we can all kick our golf anxiety.'

Archie Rosenkrantz, who was studying Otto's now bulging eyeballs, whispered sadly, 'Otto's gonna kick anxiety about when Hugh Hefner kicks silk pyjamas.'

Otto turned toward the house three times even before he stuck a tee in the ground. He could almost hear a voice singing 'Strangers in the niiiight!'

'There ain't nobody watching you!' Archie said nervously.

'Ol' blue eyes don't scare me!' Otto said courageously.

'Scoobie doobie doo, you putz!' Renfield said merrily.

Otto Stringer jerked the Top-Flite dead left. It caromed off Sidney Blackpool's golf cart and ricocheted back into the shin of Archie Rosenkrantz who couldn't duck as fast as the younger men.

'Oh, my God!' Otto wailed. 'I'm as useless as Ronald Reagan's right ear!'

Archie Rosenkrantz limped it off for a few moments before saying, 'Tell you what, Otto. Let's go to the bar and schmooz. I ain't never been much for blood sports.'

After they changed shoes, Otto headed back to the lobby to check the membership roster for celebrities. When he found Archie and Sidney Blackpool in the bar, he said, 'Does Gregory Peck come here?'

'Naw,' Archie said. 'He might've when the club was new. No more.'

'Saw the Chairman's name,' Otto said.

'He don't play golf,' said Archie. 'Maybe eats in the dining room once in a while. I think he got mad cause somebody told him not to bring Spiro Agnew around no more.'

'So who else you got here?' Otto asked.

'Lots a people whose names begin with R-O-S-E-N and G-O-L-D,' Archie said. 'Let's get you a drink.'

They put away the first cocktail before the waiter had time to ring up the check for Archie to sign. 'Hey, kid,' he said to the bartender, 'only one ice cube. Whaddaya think this is, a club for the *goyim*? You wanna work Thunderbird or Eldorado maybe?'

The bartender grinned and dumped two ice cubes, pouring more bourbon.

'Less ice than this scuttled the *Titanic*,' said Archie.

'This a Jewish club?' Otto asked.

'Whaddaya think, kid?' said Archie. 'Do I look like Henry Cabot Lodge? This club was built by Jews when they wouldn't let 'em in Thunderbird. I heard they even turned down Jack Benny.

Nowadays they might keep a few Jews but they ain't allowed to drop kippers on the greens and they gotta tie building blocks to their foreskins till they stretch. Gotta drop their drawers before they even get on the driving range, I hear.'

'I thought if you just had enough dough, you were like the big monkey, go anywhere you want.'

'You got a lot to learn, kid. Where do you guys belong, anyway?'

'Well, we don't actually belong to a club, exactly.'

'We're cops from L.A.P.D.,' Sidney Blackpool said.

'Yeah?' Archie said. 'I played a few games with two a your deputy chiefs one time. Over at Hillcrest.'

'Is it nice as this?'

'Sure. Gimme your business card. I'll have you over some time.'

'No movie stars around here, huh?' Otto was checking out the people coming from lunch.

'Maybe see Lucille Ball. Her husband's a good golfer.'

'They live here?' said Otto.

'Naw, they live in Thunderbird.'

'Why doesn't he belong to Thunderbird?'

'He's a Jew. He lives there, but he's a member a *this* club.'

'Look here, Archie,' Otto said. 'We play in Griffith Park with a bunch a cops. Among 'em there's two Mexicans, a brother, and a Jew. Now, you tell me if we all win the California lottery we can't join a fancy country club together.'

'People say they wanna be with their own kind, kiddo,' Archie said.

'But they're cops. They *are* my kind!' said Otto.

'You little *mensch*,' Archie said. 'If you could figure out a golf swing that quick you'd be the best fat golfer since Billy Casper.'

Otto was truly amazed. 'A few million bucks can't get your leg over the wall if you're not the same *kind*?'

'Easier to get a leg over the Berlin Wall,' Archie Rosenkrantz said. 'Heading west. How about another drink, kiddo? With one ice cube.'

THE CADDY

Simon Raven

'This is Martin Lash,' said the lean Brigadier, 'from Holland. I knew you wouldn't mind a three-ball.'

I hate three-balls, as my face made very plain.

'We must not be selfish,' said the lean Brigadier, flexing one shank and then the other under his plus-twos; 'we must be civil to foreigners: common market and all that crap. But you needn't worry what you say in front of him. Rather unusually for an educated Dutchman, he does not speak English. Just smile at him from time to time – that's all I'm asking.'

'That and a three-ball,' I said, grinning thinly at Martin Lash: 'he'll hold us up like the very devil.'

'Oh no. I'm getting him a caddy. You don't want one, I take it?'

'I can't afford one.'

'Good, I thought not. It would have been inconvenient.'

'Inconvenient?'

'I'm not having one either,' said the Brigadier, 'although I usually do. You'll see why not later on.'

Martin Lash was one of those men like a barrel surmounted by a croquet ball and supported by two buckets. He had been turning a polite po-face from one to the other of us during our conversation, but now showed signs of becoming restive.

'Let's get on with it,' said the Brigadier, as if duty and not pleasure were in prospect. He waved a hand towards the Caddy Master's hut. A wiry ephebe emerged: he wore a long and ragged black jerkin of indeterminate material above baggy grey trousers which ended just below the knee: his calves and feet were bare.

'This is Saul Bax,' said the Brigadier: and to Lash, 'Saul . . . Bax
. . . Caddy.'

Bax very slightly bowed his bullet head. Lash, who seemed to
have got the message, nodded his appreciation and handed his
very heavy and elaborate bag to sinewy (perhaps 16 years old)
Saul Bax.

'Showy foreign rubbish,' said the Brigadier.

'Aye, Master,' said Saul Bax.

We played the first, a short par 4, towards some ugly breeding
boxes (the only nasty sight on the course) which marked the end
of the town. The Brigadier was keeping a card: Lash had a 4 at
the first (a very lucky one), the Brigadier had a 5, and I had a
scruffy 6. So Lash had the honour on the second tee, where we now
turned and began to play away from the breeders (in a northerly
direction towards Sandwich), having the first fairway on our left
and the sea shore on our right. Lash sliced heavily. His ball bal-
looned up against the East Wind and fell, almost abreast of where
we stood but a long way from us, on to the pebbled beach.

'You go with Mr Lash, Saul,' said the Brigadier after both he
and I had managed to drive moderately straight, 'and try to find
his ball. No point the rest of us coming.'

'Aye, Master,' said Bax.

When we were alone, the Brigadier started to become conspira-
torial.

'Met him in Amsterdam,' he said. 'Interesting name. Invited him
over.

'Who is that caddy?' I said. 'Is he too skint to buy shoes, poor
chap?'

'On the contrary, Saul Bax is very well provided for,' said the
lean Brigadier, swaying from his pins to his crackly physog in the
East Wind which blew from the sea. 'For that very reason he
doesn't often work here, and so you won't have seen him before.
As for his feet, I suppose he likes to go with them bare.' He paused.
'Lee shore this morning: splendid day for wrecking.'

'For what?'

'You surely knew that the inhabitants of this coast were famous
for wrecking? You're a literary chap – Defoe says a great deal

about it in his *Tour Round the Island of Great Britain*. When ships were driven ashore on a day like today, the gangs would turn out from Walmer, Deal and Sandwich and butcher the crews for the booty. By the end of the 17th century the law got a bit of a hold: but residual gangs of wreckers operated from the dunes and the marshes until the end of the 18th century and even later.'

Martin Lash and Saul Bax reappeared. Both shook their heads. At the end of the second hole the Brigadier scored a 5 for himself and me, and a dash for Lash.

'What system are you using to score?' I asked.

'It doesn't much matter. Just filling this in for the sake of it.'

'We might at least be serious about the match,' I said, 'even if it is a three-ball.'

'Oh yes. We're very serious indeed. You'll see. Won't he, Saul?' the Brigadier called to Bax.

'Aye, Master,' said Bax.

As the round proceeded, Lash, who was plainly not used to such conditions, became wilder and wilder in his strokes. Whithersoever he propelled his ball, the faithful Bax went with him, and was surprisingly often successful in finding it. During these interludes the Brigadier continued his account of the local wreckers.

'Out of the dunes,' he said, 'leaving a look-out in case the Excise Men stuck their noses in – out of the dunes, on to the beach, hack the sailormen to bits with old iron and cutlasses – Russians, Germans, French, Dutch, or even English, what the hell? – and fetch the loot back into the marshes just down the coast, between here and Sandwich. It must have been just such a day as this in late August, 1782 – warmer of course but just as windy. This time they set a woman to watch, as they sometimes did when men were short. I'll show you where they posted her, later.'

Lash and Bax rejoined us. Lash was allowed to drop his ball and we all played up from a dip (mercifully windless) on to a plateau green on a bank which merged into the beach. Lash held a single putt.

'Give him 4 then,' said the Brigadier; 'as I say, it doesn't much matter.'

From the next tee, which was adjacent to the previous green,

Lash hooked with the wind off the sea. He and Bax tramped into a wilderness of long, spiked grasses.

'One of the crew escaped,' said the Brigadier. 'He ran over this very spot. Desperate. No golf course then. Just that clinging, spiteful grass – like the stuff Lash and Saul are in now. Only the marshes beyond. No nice trim fields like today . . . Any luck, Saul?' he called. 'No? Then let's get on. As it's such a bloody day and Mister Lash is having such a rotten time, we'll cut over to the thirteenth tee and start back home.'

'Aye, Master,' said Saul Bax.

Martin Lash, playing last off the thirteenth tee (and now facing back in the direction of the Club House), sliced his ball with his horrible, hefty, heavy swing. The East Wind gathered it and escorted it well over the Ancient Highway, which ran parallel (more or less) to the thirteenth fairway.

'Now watch out,' said the Brigadier. For the first time he accompanied Lash and Bax on their search, and beckoned me to follow with him.

'The watching woman spotted the running sailor,' said the Brigadier. 'A Dutch sailor, as it turned out. She gave a whistle towards the shore, but of course it didn't carry against the wind. She brandished a rusty pruning hook. But the Hollander disarmed her, thick, tough wench though she was. And then, because as well as being thick and tough she was juicy, had it up with her skirts and off with her maidenhood. And then strangled her to teach her obedience, and went on his way. Through the marshes. And was picked up by the King's Men in Sandwich. He didn't, of course, speak a word of English, but they soon enough twigged what he'd been about, because on this occasion the wreckers made common cause with the Sandwich Watch, wanting vengeance as they did for their look-out girl, her raped and strangled.

'There's a stone to her memory just over there', said the Brigadier, 'just to the east of the Ancient Highway.'

A handsome, grey stone, slightly and elegantly shouldered. From behind it a black mass of a screaming young woman rose up and with her talons rent the face of Martin Lash to tatters.

The woman vanished with a kind of squelch. Saul Bax laid

Lash's clubs on the ground beside Lash's body, and eyed both as if making a calculation.

'Take him away to Mary, Saul,' said the Brigadier; 'his clubs as well. Mister Raven and I don't want to be buggered up with them the rest of the way home.'

'Aye, Master,' said Saul Bax. Having concluded his survey of the load, he slung the bag of clubs over one shoulder and the body of Lash over the other, and trotted away on his bare feet over the fields (where the marshes had been once and in parts were still) towards the Cinq Port of Sandwich.

'A local boy, you see,' said the Brigadier; 'he knows the way.'

We approached the stone.

'You can't read it any longer. The letters are too worn,' said the Brigadier; 'but the Department of Works has kindly provided a crib.'

Near the stone a modest green notice (white-lettered) informed us that:

BY THIS STONE
IN AUGUST, 1782,
MARY BAX
AGED 23 YEARS and NINE MONTHS
WAS MURDERED BY MARTIN LASH,
A FOREIGNER
WHO WAS EXECUTED FOR THE SAME

'No bloody nonsense in those days,' the Brigadier said.

'But surely', I observed, 'this Martin Lash, with whom we've been playing, he can't be the man named here.'

'Oh no. A descendant, perhaps. Although the name is a happy coincidence,' said the Brigadier, 'it doesn't really matter to Mary Bax, in her vault near St Clement's . . . where her brother is even now bringing her the food of her revenge. Since he's the man of the house, you see, he carries the game-bag. She just does the killing and finds her own way home.'

'Leaving with a squelch,' I said, remembering. 'Are you sure Lash was dead?'

'Doesn't really matter. Either way, they'll share him together in their vault. So long as it's a foreigner (as this notice you see expresses the case) it's all right with them. A foreigner like Lash – that one or this. Only if there's a long shortage of foreigners does Saul carry off an Englishman, so I make it my business to keep them well supplied with what they prefer. For the good name of the Club. We can't have Englishmen, let alone our own Members, vanishing into the earth.'

'How do they know . . . when their kind of prey is available?'

'I tell 'em. There's a little hole through which you can talk into the vault by St Clement's. "Saul, Saul," I say, "Mary, oh Mary, you will have a visitor tomorrow. Come and collect him" (or *"her"* – they are in no way sexist) "at the usual time."'

'But won't someone miss him, sooner or later, someone back in Holland?'

'All busybodies will be told that Lash left this afternoon for Rye, where he has a booking at a reputable hotel. His hired car will be found parked on the road on the other side of Hythe. No Lash in it. No clubs. Total disappearance and mystery. I don't think – do you? – that the Police will look in the Bax family vault near St Clement's.'

'How did such a family come to have a vault?'

'They made a lot of money out of wrecking.'

'Why', I enquired, 'did you invite me this morning?'

'You're an author. I want you to write an account of this business. Write an account, and send it to me – for publication around 2050 AD, long after you and I are safely dead. I'll see to that in my will. For the record, you understand.'

'I understand,' I said.

'And just add as a postscript', said the lean Brigadier, with a thin-lipped giggle, 'that I hope to get a lot of Japs playing here before long. That shouldn't be difficult – they're swarming over half the courses in the country. A shower of Japs, on some business hospitality caper – that should keep Saul and Mary happy for a very long time,' the Brigadier said.

GOLF IN A NUTSHELL

Frank Muir

Golf – which is pronounced by people who earn over fifty thousand a year or own over fifty acres of land 'goff' – is a game.

It is played with a stick and a ball and is rather like playing horseless polo or solo hockey.

The sticks, which come in bundles like long bits of firewood, have a tool fixed to the bottom end. Some sticks have metal blades for digging sand out of pits and spraying it over an area of grass; some are aerodynamically designed blocks of wood so shaped that when they whizz past the ball it is blown harmlessly off its little peg, or 'tee'.

The hired assistant who prepares the 'tee' is called the 'caddy'.

The ball used in playing the game of golf is called a 'golf ball'. It is white, dimpled like a bishop's knees, and is the size of small mandarin oranges or those huge pills which vets blow down the throats of constipated cart-horses.

American golfers keep losing their ball in the Middle West or Florida and they are experimenting with putting a little radio transmitter inside it so that they can track it by its bleep. Such devices are of no interest to the British because Britain is a much smaller place to search for a ball, and most British golf balls, like most British dogs, rarely move more than a few yards from their owner's feet.

When a person strolls across the grass in front of a 'golfer' who is about to aim a blow at his golf ball with his stick, it is usual for the golfer to shout 'fore!' This is old Scottish politeness. It indicates to the stroller how many times the 'golfer' reckons he will have to

hit his golf ball before it gets near enough to the stroller to endanger him.

A game of golf is usually played between two, sometimes four, friends. Each player tries to urge his golf ball into a special hole in the grass by tapping it with one of his bundle of sticks. When the ball eventually drops into the hole the golfer remembers the number of whacks it took him and, if his friend is watching, writes that number down on his scorecard. After doing this 18 times the friends add up their scores to find the winner. As in receiving a prison sentence, or the news of a multiple birth of offspring, a low number is hoped for. After working out who is the winner, the losers all say 'Well done!' and silently accompany their ex-friend back to the clubhouse.

It is the ambition of every 'golfer' to urge his golf ball down the hole with just one hit of his stick. He will then become famous, be promoted, become rich, speak of 'goff', and buy a house which backs on to a 'golf course'. Then when people ask him what sort of a home he has he is able to boast: 'There are fairways at the bottom of our garden.'

THE LURE OF GOLF

Chris Plumridge

A few aeons ago, shortly after the era of the firmament and the crawlies, there wasn't a lot going on at weekends. I mean there were no trips out into the country with family for a picnic, no visiting stately homes, and there wasn't much sport on television either. No, it must have been pretty dull when the Friday night hooter went and early man trudged back to the cave. Faced with the prospect of 48 hours of domesticity it may well have been that our hero, using some excuse like taking the pterodactyl for a quick flight round the block, would have nipped out for a few hours in the countryside. While he was there he may also have picked up a stick lying on the ground, swished it through the air and listened to that satisfying 'whoosh' sound. After a while he would have become slightly bored with just making 'whooshing' noises and espying a nice, round pebble on the pathway would have taken a swipe at it. No doubt he would have missed the first time but eventually he would have made contact and sent the pebble winging off into the wide blue yonder.

It was a few thousand years later that pebble-hitting of this nature really caught on and somebody had the bright idea of calling it golf. Since then the game has spread like wildfire, to the extent that there is hardly a country in the world that has not succumbed to its lure.

So what is it about this exercise with club and ball that affects man, woman and child so strongly? Is it in fact 'a good walk spoiled' (Mark Twain) or 'a game devised by the devil with instruments ill-suited for its purpose' (W. S. Churchill)? Or is it a little like malaria in that once you have been bitten, the parasite remains with you forever?

There are a few deep thinkers who have attempted to analyse why the golf virus attacks them so forcefully. The game's fascination, in their opinion, lies in the fact that whatever else may be going on, it all comes down to you, the club and the ball. There is no opponent outplaying you to such an extent that you may not hit the ball at all, as can occur in snooker; there are no umpires or referees who, in your opinion, would be better equipped with a white stick than a whistle, such is the blindness of some of their decisions; and there are no team-mates who regard your brilliance with such disdain that they don't allow you to touch the ball for almost the entire match.

Once you step on to the course you may be playing against par, your opponent, the elements and the topography of the land but your chief opponent is yourself. This is the game's enduring appeal and why it reveals far more of a person's character than any psychiatrist could worm out in umpteen sessions on an expensive Manhattan couch. Could, for example, a man who breaks his club after a bad shot and then storms off the course after the round without buying a drink be trusted to keep a cool head if Amalgamated Rivet makes a hostile bid? Or could a woman who giggled after missing a short putt be considered a suitable wife and/or mother of your children? Golf not only poses the questions but also provides the answers.

Of course there are other reasons for golf's popularity. The setting where it is played is one of its greatest appeals. Whether you are playing on one of the most famous championship courses in the world or merely on a small, nine-hole layout in some quiet backwater, you are in harmony with nature. The feel and smell of the grass, the whiff of fresh air in your nostrils and the sound of a lark soaring overhead all combine to produce a heady cocktail of natural beauty. That is not to say that all golfers are budding naturalists – far from it. Most golfers couldn't tell the difference between a fescue bent and a Bermuda broad-leaf, a red-backed shrike from a peewit. Indeed, any golfer who displays such knowledge of these matters is regarded with the highest suspicion.

Golfers are aware of their surroundings but view them as part of the game's bounty.

Where golfers do have a rapport with the land is how it would be best suited for golf. In other words, inside every golfer there is a golf course architect trying to get out. Course architecture enables a golfer to work on the broadest canvas available to an artist and also to leave a lasting monument to his genius – it is the ultimate ego trip.

There are thousands of golf courses throughout the world, some still in the early stages of construction, others which have been played over for centuries. All of them provide, or will provide, a degree of pleasure to every player who sets foot on them, whether it be for the sheer challenge they present or simply as a place for fresh air and exercise. There are courses set on parkland, meadowland, on mountains and beside the sea. Some have even been constructed on deserts. Some courses are awash with water hazards, others swarming with bunkers, some will have tree-lined fairways, others with hardly a tree in sight, some will be inordinately long, others extremely short. Each will be different so that a golfer could spend a lifetime travelling the world and still find something fresh and stimulating. Of course, there are also degrees of stimulation and this is where the golfer has to make a judgment as to what constitutes a great course, a good course or an indifferent one. This judgment should not be based on how the golfer fared through the round – a bad score doesn't necessarily mean a bad course – but should be formed objectively. For example, would the course provide equal enjoyment to all golfers, no matter what their standard? Could the golfer, at the end of the round, sit down and have instant recall of every hole? Did the course draw upon the full repertoire of strokes, from controlled drives to delicate pitches? Did the holes cause the golfer to think and assess what was required before each shot? Finally, and perhaps most importantly so far as the average golfer is concerned, was it a course where he could play happily for the rest of his days without staleness ever dulling the pleasure?

These are the criteria for a memorable course and the game has been fortunate in having course architects who have imbued these fundamentals with a creative touch which elevates their designs above the rest. These courses stand as memorials to their talents and have assumed the mantle of greatness; even so, nearly all the courses which have achieved fame or notoriety owe their standing to a strip of land hard by the coast near a small Fifeshire fishing town.

St Andrews is the original masterpiece. Some people say that God was so preoccupied with the business of Creation that he devised the Old Course as a practice ground for the Real Thing. The truth is somewhat more ordinary: the Old Course simply emerged and evolved. The basic design has not changed over the centuries and its problems are still severe despite the modernisation of equipment and the improved physical powers of the current top players. The legacy that the Old Course has left the game is probably best encapsulated in three holes, the 11th, called the High Hole, a short hole of 172 yards, the 14th, or Long Hole, at 567 yards, and the 17th, the Road Hole, a par four of 461 yards. These holes have been a major influence on golf course design, providing a source of inspiration for architects throughout the world. The Road Hole is, in this writer's humble opinion, the finest hole in the world. It has been drawing the metaphorical blood of golfers from the era of Tom Morris to the era of Tom Watson. Some of its teeth have been pulled: the removal of the old railway sheds to be replaced by the Old Course Hotel which looks like a clothes chest with all the drawers left open; and the resurfacing of the road itself may have caused some spinning in the more notable graves up in the local churchyard, but even in this age of power hitting the Road Hole can still exact savage retribution.

The hole is a marvellous example of the use of angles to confuse and frustrate the golfer. From the tee, the presence of the out-of-bounds on the right makes the player instinctively aim away to the left. But the further left the tee shot, the more imperceptible becomes the target of the green. And what a target! The front of the green rises alarmingly to a narrow shelf and again, the angle of the green in relation to the approach shot means that any stroke slightly overhit will skitter through on to the dreaded road. That really should be enough, but nature conjured up one more impossible trick in the shape of the Road bunker on the left of the green, 'eating its way into its very vitals' as Bernard Darwin once described it.

It may be of passing interest that the 17th at St Andrews could have been the 21st. In the middle of the 18th century it was generally accepted that the golfers of St Andrews were leaders in the development of the game and in 1764, the Society of St Andrews Golfers changed its course to eighteen holes. Prior to that the golfers played 11 holes going 'out' and then returned on the same route playing 11 holes home, so a round comprised 22 holes. The Society decided to make the first four holes into two and thus a round became 18 holes. For the majority of golfers, designing and building golf courses is something to dream about by the fireside on a winter's evening. The architectural profession is now dominated by former players whose careers have come to a close but can still be involved in the higher reaches of the game by designing a course which will eventually stage a championship.

Where the ordinary mortal can dabble in this field is by becoming Chairman of the Green Committee at his local club. Once they reach this post they very often set about altering the course to suit their own game. Thus a bunker that has always ensnared their tee shot at the first is mysteriously filled in and grassed over, and so the process goes on elsewhere on the course. This is very dangerous stuff since the Chairman is probably totally unqualified to make such changes and his successor is likely to institute some completely different alterations. Eventually, if this is allowed to happen, the course bears little resemblance to the original and becomes an amateurish mish-mash of mistaken intentions.

One of the game's vicarious pleasures is that it enables the ordinary player to tread in the footsteps of the immortals. Other sportsmen may imagine themselves performing on the sacred turf of Lord's, Wembley or Wimbledon but they are unlikely actually to do so. Golfers can not only play the courses where the great championships take place, they can find themselves in exactly the same place where a Nicklaus or a Ballesteros has been previously and may, occasionally, be able to emulate them.

This too is another of golf's eternal tugs – that unexpected melding of muscle and sinew which contrives to deliver the club-head to the ball at exactly the right angle and direction and produce a shot of staggering virtuosity. No matter how badly a golfer may have performed, there is always one perfect stroke which will bring him back again. This is part of golf's great delusion, the ability it has to 'con' the golfer into believing that the one perfect shot is the rule rather than the exception.

This applies to how a golfer scores as well. A golfer may go round regularly in a score somewhere between 92 and 100 but one day he has one of those rounds when everything goes right. He will chip in a couple of times, hole a number of lengthy putts, the odd drive will hit a tree and bounce back on to the fairway and lo and behold, he has gone round in 85. This golfer no longer regards himself as a 90 shooter, he is now an 85 shooter and any rounds above that score are just 'off days'.

All golfers believe there is some hidden secret to playing effective golf. A minute adjustment to the little finger of the left hand will have them hitting the ball miles further and the course record will be a formality. This accounts for the vast number of golf books published each year carrying such titles as 'How to lower your handicap in one easy move' or 'You can become a better player overnight'. These offerings are usually fronted by a top name professional who imparts his advice to an unsuspecting public which fails to realise that the professional has forearms like a stevedore and spends every waking minute hitting golf balls. Despite these differences, golfers still try and mimic the professionals' methods, often with disastrous results.

Another area where golfers demonstrate an almost incredible naivety is in the equipment they use. Again, most golfers believe there is an easy route to improvement simply by purchasing a set of clubs or using a particular brand of ball. The equipment manufacturers have not been slow to exploit the gullible nature of golfers and promote their products through some of the most preposterous claims ever conceived by any copywriter in the history of advertising. All manufacturers claim (a) that their clubs hit the ball further and (b) that their ball flies further. Distance and more distance is the message of the modern age.

So how far has golf come in the 250 years since it caught on in Scotland? The answer is, quite a distance. It was a fortunate accident that golf took root in Scotland since anyone who has lived there for any length of time will know that it is an excellent place to emigrate from at the first opportunity. Incessant rain, howling winds and a sort of clammy, cold fog called 'haar' make golf in Scotland a true Pilgrim's Progress, a tempering of the spirit from which all players will emerge the better. Faced with such conditions it is hardly surprising that the Scots left their native heath in droves and set about colonising the world with golf. The game took root in America with a Scot and no matter where you travel in the world, if two or more Scotsmen are gathered in the name of Old Tom Morris you can bet your last bawbee there will be a golf course nearby.

The general consensus among non-golfers is that golfers are a little unbalanced, if not completely mad. There may be some truth in this but such an analysis fails to consider the fact that golf gives its devotees much more than most games, and therefore its participants do become obsessive about it.

In truth, golf is really like life and the people who play it reflect the society in which they live. Thus it attracts the super-achievers who see the course record as just another obstacle to be overcome. It has its officious watchdogs who know every procedure and rule in the book. It has its loners and introverts who love golf because they can play without the need of an opponent or partner. It has its brash, hail-fellow-well-met types who love it for exactly the opposite reason. It has its scientists and technicians who can theorise for hours on some esoteric point in the swing. It has its gamblers for whom life is incomplete without several bets running concurrently. It has those who dress as if for a funeral and those who dress as if for a carnival in Rio. It has its misogynists who regard the golf club as one of the few places left where the tramp of the monstrous regiment of women can go unheard and it has the inevitable mixing of the sexes when love of the game can result in many a variation of mixed foursomes.

On such evidence, the only really surprising thing about golf is that it is not played by everybody.

IN DISPRAISE OF GOLF

John Ebdon

I make no pretence about it. Devoted though I am to all ball games, including Association Football at international level when I am motivated by chauvinism, I dislike golf intensely. Possibly the reason is Freudian and stems from unhappy memories of members of my family who were addicted to the pursuit. A maiden aunt of mine was of their number. She was totally resistible.

Known as The Aunt, grim-faced and never happier than when striding aggressively across divers links bellowing 'fore', she was a large lady, well endowed both front and rear, and with child-bearing hips which were never put to the test. These were encased by a thick tweed skirt of tartan design secured under duress by a large safety pin. Privately I thought that it would be unwise to breed from her, an opinion patently endorsed by all males post puberty for she enjoyed a single status until the age of eighty-one when she was courted and won by a nonagenarian suffering from acute myopia and clearly resigned to the fact that he was one of nature's fall guys. Fortunately, and doubtless frightened by the macabre experience, he died intestate and incontinent within eighteen months of the unholy matrimony. However, in her earlier years and for a reason which still escapes me – unless it was unrequited sadism on her part – The Aunt took it upon herself to introduce me to the game of golf, or, as she pronounced it 'goff', while staying as a house guest with my mother and father during the school holidays.

In my eighth year and at a time when I was enthusiastically accepting my father's tuition on the basics of passing a rugby ball and keeping a straight bat, she presented me with a third-hand putter and two scarred golf balls and commanded my father's gardener to make a hole in the immaculate lawn with a trowel. Apprehensive of my father's wrath at the desecration of his turf but still more fearful of The Aunt with whom only the bravest or the foolhardy would argue, reluctantly he obeyed.

'That's the ticket, Gosling,' she bellowed as he completed the enormity, and straightway launched upon a course of instruction, breathing heavily and looming over me with her feet astride and her arms akimbo. Thus intimidated, both my confidence and any latent talent I might have had for the sport quickly evaporated. 'No boy, no,' she thundered as repeatedly I missed the target by several feet. 'Stroke it! Stroke it! Balls should be stroked, not snatched! Now try again, boy, try again. And, Gosling! Stop sniggerin' – you're putting him orf!'

I wished her to perdition. As Gosling confirmed to me later, 'She be a right ole besom that there Miss Edith, Master John. Orter be put down I reckon.' Mercifully she departed a few days later to embark upon a walking expedition in the Sudan where no doubt she terrorised the natives: but she left her mark upon me. For weeks after my return to school I tossed and turned in my dormitory bed dreaming that I was battering her head with a niblick.

The Aunt may have been the first of my relatives to alienate me from the game, but there were others who made me equally wary of the pastime, albeit for different reasons: in short, for the possible effect it can have on one's physique. One such kinsman was my Great-uncle Piers.

It was quite by chance that I was given an unexpected and startling reminder of that worthy. Flicking between the covers of my late father's 1928 edition of *Wisden* in search of the statistics of one Jack Ebdon, upon whom greatness was thrust when he was twice invited to play for Somerset, but who failed to reach double figures in all four innings, a faded photograph of Great-uncle Piers came butterflying out of the pages and landed face upward on the carpet. Closer scrutiny revealed that the camera had recorded him for posterity leaning upon a mashie before the Club House at Sunningdale, accoutred in plus-fours and topped by what at first sight appeared to be a deflated pizza. Subserviently hovering in the sepia background was a diminutive caddy bowed down under the weight of a golf bag and plainly in need of a new truss; but it was my uncle's expression which demanded attention. It was vacant. Unseeing eyes stared glassily into the camera lens while the suspicion of an idiot smile played upon his lips. Not that this was out of the ordinary. Great-uncle Piers was not the brightest of men.

Baptised Piers Edgecombe but known affectionately as Pipey, for reasons which in the interest of decency must remain confidential, he was a stout, pink-faced Devonian with deep blue, permanently surprised eyes who meandered through life with the air of a man who knew vaguely where he was but was unsure why, and who felt that he should be somewhere else but could not remember where. He was, as they would say in Yorkshire, 'yonderly'. Nevertheless, on this occasion his traits were more marked than usual; and with good reason. He had, it transpired, been struck forcefully on the left temple by a competitor's errant ball whilst contemplating a stymie on the thirteenth green. Some ten seconds later when his brain eventually registered the hurt, he staggered to a nearby bunker and collapsed in an untidy heap. However, true to the tradition of his class and public school upbringing, and conscious that he must never make a fuss in public, he took a liberal libation from his hip flask, manfully regained an upright stance and allowed his caddy to assist him to the Club House. Once there he accepted condolences and further restoratives from sympathetic well-wishers and resolved to pose before the building in order to dispel any rumours that he had been maimed irreparably by a fellow member and so draw unwelcome publicity to the Club: hence the photograph. However, family history records that the braggadocio was to cost him dear.

Within days it became clear that his mental abilities – always below par even when he was enjoying rude physical health – had deteriorated alarmingly. On the Saturday following the incident he caused consternation by lighting his pipe during a service of Holy Matrimony in the Parish Church of Guildford as the bride said 'she would'; in nearby Bramley he was long remembered by a minor Canon whose sherry he topped up with soda water; and a week later, en route for luncheon at the Athenaeum, when accosted by a lady of easy virtue in Curzon Street he afforded her considerable thought by advising her to go away as he was a respectably married woman.

Uncharitable relations who catalogued these happenings theorised that Great-uncle Piers's demeanour had nothing to do with being hit on the head by a golf ball. He was, they opined, already well on the way to becoming unhinged without further assistance. Even my father, the fairest of men, allowed that golf should not be held responsible for Pipey's condition. It could, he conjectured, just as easily have been caused by a misdirected hockey or cricket ball, or during a game of rugby; but even he failed to convince me and I continued to look upon golf with deep misgivings. Moreover, unintentionally my father fanned the flames of my disenchantment.

I admired my father hugely. An aficionado of most sports, equally competent with both bat and ball, and no mean performer on the squash and tennis courts, he was a stern but scrupulously just man who instilled in me at an early age the importance of being a good loser. As I was seldom allowed the luxury of being a good winner, this advice was to prove invaluable. Also, as befitted an officer and a gentleman, he nearly always retained full control of his emotions. Indeed, there was but one particular which caused him to abandon this admirable English quality: golf.

I was first made aware of this peccadillo in Le Touquet in Northern France, where we repaired yearly en famille in those far-off days before the war clouds lowered over Europe in the late nineteen-thirties. My mother enjoyed the Continent. My father did not. Instinctively he mistrusted foreigners and when abroad opened his mouth solely to remove his pipe or to admit food. This he disliked on principle. However, in his eyes Le Touquet had one redeeming feature and a good enough reason for him to give his blessing on our annual pilgrimage. It had a golf course.

Daily, and in the highest of spirits having pushed aside his brioche and jam and by gesture and grunt had had them replaced with *le bacon and eggs*, he would bid us a smiling goodbye, wish us the happiest of days and, full of expectant joy, sally forth to the links. Three hours later, much of which it emerged had been spent lowering the depth of a bunker and clouding the sun with sand or replacing divots in the Gallic turf, he returned a changed man.

The metamorphosis was horrid to behold. Gone was the twinkle in his eyes, no longer were the lips prepared to part in a ready smile, and the spring had gone out of his step. Much of luncheon was spent in a pregnant silence as he stared even more morosely than usual at the chef's offering. Nervously sipping at my Evian in an attempt to break the conversational deadlock, gauchely I asked him if he had had a good morning.

Slowly he lifted his eyes from his untouched platter and looked at me across the table without any sign of paternal affection. 'Sometimes', he said acidly, 'it is better to keep one's mouth shut and let people think you're a fool than to open it and remove any possible shadow of doubt.'

Fortuitously Providence, in the guise of a French crook, saved us from further misery. Three days after his initial onslaught on the greens his clubs were stolen and after a brief period during which he railed about the iniquities of the Gauls in particular and foreigners in general, collectively we returned to sanity. No longer did he call me to task for the slightest misdemeanour nor snap at my mother and it was with unrestrained joy that once again we heard him singing 'Keep the Home Fires Burning' as he lathered himself with carbolic soap and performed his morning ablutions. But I did not quickly forget those seventy-two hours in Le Touquet when the 'yips' from which he suffered when putting were also exhibited by me.

I loved my father dearly. He was a good, kind, and normally a considerate person, but as I discovered, his Achilles' heel was golf. Perhaps he tried too hard to excel at the game and lost his sense of proportion. Certainly he continued in the hunt for excellence until well into his late seventies: but one thing for sure. More than any other man I know, he demonstrated aptly the maxim of P. G. Wodehouse, who described golf as 'a game in which ambition outruns achievement'.

These are the reminiscences of adolescence when every encounter with golfers visibly worsened my acne, but even with my advancing years I found little to endear me to the game and its devotees. Constantly I was reminded of their religion and fervour, and continue to be so.

In the region of North London where I live, I look upon the open spaces of Northwick Park playing fields. The area serves a multitude of purposes. During all seasons men and women of pensionable age, some track-suited and wearing knitted hats with pom-poms on them and risking cardiac fatigue, puff and wheeze their ways around the periphery, steaming as they jog. Others, more circumspectly, exercise their dogs, unleashing them to chase the gulls which winter always brings to the ill-drained turf, or command them to 'Sit!' or 'Stay!' Most do neither but run away with pink lolling tongues to violate the nearest bushes. However, when the grass is long and the chill has gone from the land, the fields are the haunt of every sex-orientated couple in Christendom and many a moan and groan of ecstasy may be heard in the fading light. But when it has been sheared to within an inch of the ground, the grassland becomes an arena for aspiring Ballesteroses and Woosnams.

From first light onward these zealots may be seen attempting to hit balls into the middle distance with unwavering concentration, and the air is filled with the swish of drivers and the click of club-heads engaging their targets. And when the shadows lengthen and the sun weakens I watch them leave, red-faced and happy, and with their departure and the field empty, I go forth in search of spoils.

I am seldom disappointed. On a good day I return with a bag full of plastic tees and, on average, half a dozen balls lost to their owners. Some are yellow, some are white and most bear signs of wear and tear, but all are welcome at the Sue Ryder shop to which I take them and where they are turned into coin to help the ungolfing needy. However, not all players appreciate this altruism.

It was just before dusk on a late August day that I reaped my greatest harvest. Head bowed toward the ground and my hands clasped behind my back, thoughtfully I sauntered across the fields in search of booty. Success came quickly. Within thirty yards I came upon a ball emblazoned with the logo 'Topflite' and remarkable for its excellent condition. Five paces later I happened upon another similarly inscribed, and then another . . . and another . . . and another.

Working methodically and pausing only to give thanks for the unexpected windfall, I pocketed the lot. Thus, deeply engrossed, it was only when I stooped to pouch the eleventh trophy that I was made aware of a major hitch in the proceedings. As my fingers reached out to pluck the ball from its resting place, noiselessly and unheralded, a pair of 12-size boots loomed into view, and stopped before it. Slowly, almost in slow motion, I straightened up and came face to face with their owner. It was a disagreeable experi-ence. He was a muscular man considerably my junior and eclipsing me in height, smelling strongly of mixed ales and with, as I was to discover, a rich command of basic Anglo-Saxon. I would not have invited him into my drawing-room.

He wasted no time on preliminaries. 'And wot', he enquired hoarsely, 'd'you think you're effing well doing, mate?' It was a rhetorical question. 'Oh yer,' he continued, warming to his subject, 'I know your sort, mate. Go round snitchin' people's balls doan-cha, yer thievin' bastard, and then bloody flog 'em, doancha? Oh yer', he reiterated, 'I know your lot. Know 'ow much these cost, mate?' he inquired, producing a similar sample from his pocket, 'well, I'll tell yer. Twenty nicker an effing dozen. Yer, that's wot you'd 'ave gottaway with if I 'adn't stopped cha – twenty nicker! Now give me me balls back and eff off – sharpish. *And*', he added, stabbing me in the stomach with a none too clean forefinger as I complied with hardly audible apologies, 'if I see you round 'ere again, mate, I'll bloody do yer. Savvy?'

I swallowed hard. 'Yes,' I said meekly, 'I savvy', and watched him go out of my life still muttering and breathing fire. I like to think that he was untypical of the golfing fraternity and wondered which Club, if any, had embraced him regardless of his handicap; but I heeded his advice. I had no wish to be done.

It was during the October of that year that the blue-rinsed lady in the Sue Ryder shop asked me why the supply of golf-balls had dried up. 'Ah,' I said lamely, and without conviction, 'I think they're out of season . . .'

Verbum Sap. Keen ornithologist though I am, in golfing parlance I remain in ignorance of birdies, albatrosses and eagles: and the term bogey still has an unpleasant connotation. Nor, despite the cajoleries of friends to whom golfing is a way of life, do I wish to be enlightened. But I admit freely that I am in the minority. Golf, according to well authenticated sources, is in the ascendancy, and in the Cotswolds, where once the cereal crops and cattle of mixed farms created the landscape, the fields are being converted into courses as local farmers cash in on this wave of increased popularity and demand. Moreover, I must concede one important point. In my opinion, golf at a professional level remains one of the few games still played in a spirit of true sportsmanship. Links are innocent of the unpleasant and unwanted scenes unfortunately so prevalent at Wimbledon, Twickenham, Wembley and (O tempora! O mores!) at Lord's. In brief, it is a pastime for genuine gentlemen: long may it remain so.

Golfers of the world, although you bore me, with my hand on my heart, I salute you! Vale!

WHY DON'T THEY PLAY GOLF?

Bill Tidy

Why is the last object left in every washing-up bowl a teaspoon? Why does the queue to which you have moved instantly freeze while the one that you have just left suddenly leaps forward? Why does the jam side of the bread always hit the deck first?

It was a neat hook on which to hang a nice little radio series and it worked quite well. The listeners received it with the half-remembered apathy that signifies a straddling of their interest without actually hitting it. Good enough for me and nothing to do with golf, but it was the very last item in the final programme which brings me to these pages.

We'd why'd every damn thing from the way the baby disappears down the plug-hole in different hemispheres to the propensity of the left shoelace to snap before its twin and there was still a three-minute end of series slot to fill.

Sport attracts serendipity and I desperately trawled the back pages looking for oddities. 'Why are there no black Olympic swimmers?' seemed to be a good one but I remembered seeing a one-legged Negro in Egypt years ago selling crocodile-skin handbags and it would be my luck for him to pick it up on the World Service. A report of a prodigious drive by Ian Botham in a pro-am charity golf tournament made me wonder why hole distances are still in yards and not metres? Hmm . . . yes, mildly interesting. Still, golf might be a case worth pursuing. Lots of anachronisms there. Professional golfers pee but caddies don't, or at least they didn't at Birkdale Open years ago when the bag carriers weren't given any toilet facilities and if some of the leading American names in the pack hadn't threatened to down clubs still wouldn't have any today. I looked for more. Golf news. The usual Americans, with a few Brits and Spaniards, were clustered at the top of the scorecard in the Charles Manson Classic or something in Florida where a complete unknown was leading the field. As ever the new phenomenon had one of those completely unlikely American names, Fuzzy Bumkoller, Norgan Spote, etc., it doesn't matter now, but what he did do was cause the blindingly obvious to leap up and dazzle me! Excitedly I went down the 136s, 137s and so on, right through to the 151s. There were (USA unless stated otherwise) Millers, Floyds, Raffertys (Ir), Langers (Ger), Takahashis (Jap), Ballesteroses (Sp) and Lyles (Sco). I thought of golfing names. Palmer, Cotton, Jacklin, Woosnam, Lema, Thomson, Lu, Trevino, Weiskopf, handles from every part of the world. Except one. Russia!

I don't mean no 'vitchs', 'skis' or 'ovs'. Every bit of rough in the USA teems with Stradivariovskys! I mean the real article, a genuine snow-on-his-balls Russian golfer! There weren't any! There was once a huge shambles called the USSR but even in that indescribable mess, where there were at first no tennis players of note, they produced them eventually. Sport was the key to a reasonable standard of living, and perhaps a bit of shoplifting at Marks and Spencer overseas, but when the whole thing fell to bits and all of the little countries escaped, still no golfers! You could say that the escapees had better things to do than working out handicaps but that applies to everyone. I had a friend, a tea biologist in Assam who played the 17th twice in one day on the old Royal Magapur with a different corpse hanging from the same branch of the big tree to the left of the green. You must come to terms with hazards, so why no Russian golfers?

I rang the then Embassy of the USSR asking for the name of the Secretary at Novogovodisk Golf Club, as I was thinking of taking up a business appointment in that fine old city and sought to become a member. I also pointed out that alcohol was my weakness and that I wasn't Jewish. Most of this was, of course, complete fabrication but in my previous dealings with the Embassy they had always lied to me and I saw no harm in a bit of Titski Tatski. Mr Petrov, third Cultural and Leisure Attaché (a lie) had no idea but made the point, which I hadn't thought of, that surely it must be criminally stupid to allow such a large area to be used occasionally by 200 or so of the privileged aristocracy when the same space could cater for 30,000 footballers and gymnasts.

Intourist were most helpful. The girl said that there were no eighteen- or nine- or even one-hole golf courses in the USSR and therefore there were no golfers. Thus far I was learning lots of things that I didn't want to know, so on an offchance I rang the Patriarch of the Estonian Church in Exile. He wasn't available but the caretaker told me amidst gales of laughter that Radio America, the Goon Show of Eastern Europe, had always insisted that there was one golf course in Russia. It was in Moscow, in the Kremlin, and all the praesidium qualified for membership as it was Crazy Golf.

Sunningdale, St Andrews and Milton Keynes municipal GCs all tried hard but none could offer an answer to my question. I could have tried the golf correspondents of the national press but it always ends up with them borrowing money so another approach was called for. The secretary of the Royal College of Surgeons assured me that there were no physical reasons preventing Russians from addressing, hitting or cursing a golf ball, so the only logical explanation for their blindness to a great sport was a mental block brought on by political brain washing. Ringing the Embassy again was out of the question so my next call was to the *Morning Star*. It all seems like ancient history now. Out-of-date names, places, blocs, but the chap who answered me was preserved in aspic. 'Russian millions have been denied access to golf by those bastards at the R and A. They could be world beaters. Look at Olga Korbet.' 'Don't talk rubbish,' I said. 'Russia's a huge place. Who could stop them building Golfograd miles from anywhere? They could have a 1000-hole golf course running alongside the railway line from . . .' He shouted 'Spy satellites!' and hung up.

How far had I got and what time was left? A couple of days and all that was established was that the USSR, Russia, CIS, call them what you like, apparently had no golf courses and consequently no players. Not even in the Coca-Cola town, built as a replica of Middle America, where spies learned to live with burgers and apple pie. Only now, too late, could I show the FBI how to

nail a Soviet agent. Ask him or her to hit a one-iron. It really was perplexing. We've got used to Chinese and Japanese golfers but they also were rare not so long ago. Why did they break through and not the Russians? Is there something about the game which frightens or appals the Slav? Does the ferocious arc of Daly's driver stir racial memories of the Boyars knout or is it because you can't pump a golfer full of steroids to any great advantage? Too much muscle and you have a clone of the famous golfing gorilla who drives *and* putts 350 yards! Or do they simply not care? No, because there were too many different kinds of folk under the old red flag to lump together so maybe it was an executive decision by Lenin. I agreed with him when he said 'Shoot all the lawyers' and am still amazed that he excluded accountants from his list, but 'Shoot all golfers' seems a bit over the top. Even sending those who played golf secretly at night to labour camps would be unkind, although it does inspire wicked images of low handi-cappers arguing over the correct stance to adopt when chipping away at a cob of salt. There are a few members in this country whom I would gladly put on the eastbound train; to be specific, those who recently refused a family lunch at their club because of improper dress. The baby was wearing denims.

The terror of my approaching deadline now made me reason that if Russians didn't or couldn't play golf at home, perhaps they might do it here in the UK. 'Find me a Russian,' I cried. 'A sporty one willing to hit a golf ball.' It was easier said than done at that time because most UK Russians were over sixty-five and legless or under sixty-five and being ballet dancers of several sexes unable to stand still for more than two seconds. Then someone suggested a student.

Inquiries at Aston University, Birmingham, produced Valery. Glory be, there he was, willing to help in his sports coat and baggy flannels. About thirty-five, slim and with that open face, surely he was a golfer! No, the interpreter said, he had never played before but had watched the game many times on television and found it relaxing. Brian, my producer, said that this is the man we are looking for and we bundled him and the interpreter into the car and headed for the local golf club.

It was a warm, windless day, with just a few couples hacking around and after introducing Valery to the professional we wandered over to the vacant tenth with a selection of clubs and balls. The pro gave Valery his ten-minute 'golf is simple' lecture and our hero nodded several times during the interpretation. A five-iron was placed in his hands and he was nudged and prodded into the address. We were impressed by his lack of nerves and exchange of Cyrillic banter with his interpreter. Valery drew a breath and then belted an imaginary ball out of sight. 'Not bad,' the pro said, 'but keep his head still.' He placed a shiny new ball at Valery's feet and nodded. Whack! It fizzed away waist high for about eighty yards. 'Tell him he's trying to kill the poor little bugger. Hit through it!'

This time only the pro saw it go. It went steepling away, dead straight for 150 yards. The pro clapped. 'Not bad. Try three or four more.' The success rate was about eighty per cent with no air shots and even the not-so-good shots going down the middle of the fairway. The driver defeated him, but with a recap from the pro on each new club he did the right thing most of the time. He remembered to keep his right elbow tucked in, left arm straight across the chest on the back swing and his head still, eyes on the ball. My commentary to the tape recorder could have been describing the pro striking, because the sound effects were crisp and sweet, so much so that the instructor felt compelled to belt a few stonkers himself as reassurance that he hadn't inadvertently passed everything he knew to the pupil.

Brian was delighted. We hadn't answered 'Why don't Russians play golf?' but at least we'd proved that they *could*, and this Russian had even done it at first touch. Perhaps he could tell us why the teaspoon stayed in the washing-up bowl or why the jam side hit the deck first? He wasn't able to but just went on hitting very decent shots till we ran out of tape. On the playback they sounded so good that we didn't have to cheat, and all that was left for a wrap was the final 'and you've never played before' between Valery and myself. This went along nicely with bits from the pro until we got to 'Do you think golf would become popular in Russia?' Valery suddenly became animated and walked off a short distance with his interpreter where they talked for a while. We felt a little concerned because it had all gone so well up to now and I wondered if I'd said something that might have been misinterpreted. 'What's the problem, Valery?' Brian called. They stopped talking and rejoined us. 'Valery feels that he could have played so much better . . .' The pro raised his hands. 'Believe me, he did exceptionally well. I've never seen a beginner hit the ball so well, so naturally . . .' The interpreter interrupted him. 'Yes, yes, he would like again to hit the ball, only properly this time, naturally, as you say!'

It was getting out of hand and Brian had to point out that we'd run out of tape, time was pressing and he had a spot of editing to do on what he was sure was going to be a very good piece of radio. We shook hands all round with the pro offering Valery a couple of free lessons if he felt that strongly about hitting the ball, or if he didn't fancy tuition there was a driving range close by where he could hammer away as long as he liked. When this was forwarded to Valery he said he would like the lessons but would he be allowed to play naturally? 'That's what teaching is about. Getting people to do things naturally, without having to think,' the pro answered, just a little huffily. 'I interfere as little as possible.'

We all shook hands again after a date was fixed and piled back into the car. Brian drove us back to Valery's lodgings, delighted with the item and a series almost wrapped up. I turned in my seat and thumbs-upped the new golfer. 'OK, Valery, you happy?' He smiled and gesticulated in return as the interpreter said, 'He is very happy, because if they allow him to play the way he wants he feels so much more comfortable than the other way.' 'What other way?' I asked. The interpreter shrugged. 'They make him play right-handed. He is left-handed.'

GOLF, MY FATHER, AND SIGMUND FREUD

Richard Condon

Whenever my wife felt particularly blue, we would get into the car and visit a golf driving range in the suburbs of New York City, where I would rent a golf stick and a bucket of balls. After settling my wife in a chair nearby I would tee up the first of the fifty balls in the bucket, then, feet apart, eyes-on-the-ball, I would measure my back-swing by the line of my shoulders and, with intent co-ordination, swing around, down and through. Every move was done by the rules of 'Power Golf', but not only did I not 'top' the ball or slice it danger-ously off course, I never succeeded in hitting it at all.

Although I would occasionally modify my stance into the rec-ommended Snead, Palmer and Nicholson positions and although I moved deliberately and with total body wisdom, I have never succeeded in hitting a golf ball. However, the effect on my wife of all this air-fanning was utterly electric. Her blues would be gone. Her laughter and her steadily pointing finger would soon draw a crowd of golfing enthusiasts who would ring themselves round me in silent respect – except that, in unison, they counted each of my swings aloud.

To be certain that my wife had been returned to her normal, merry self, I would keep trying to hit the same little ball for twenty-five to thirty swings; but hitting it was not to be, ever to be, because of my father.

Golfers of every stripe have chosen from a cornucopia of alibis concerning why they didn't score a hole-in-one every time they teed off, or why they chose to hook the ball with every drive, but it is improbable that any of them ever sought an explanation for their failures at golf in Sigmund Freud.

Fish suffer deep bruises in the fishbowl as a result of collisions with parent fish. I am no exception, but who could have predicted the awful effect the conduct of my male parent would have on my golf game?

My father was a successful lawyer, a Captain in the US Naval Reserve, and a relentlessly gregarious man. He was an intimate of Alfred E. Smith, who was to run for the presidency of the United States. All of these achievements suggest a keenly competitive personality. At social gatherings he would appear from nowhere, under an endless assortment of hats or masks, singing off-key and over-watering his drinks. He was relentlessly determined to be the life of the party patently without recourse to artificial stimulation, so that everyone there assembled would understand that his social skills and services far exceeded those of any of the other guests.

My father owned the first automobile for miles around: a Metz. My mother, small brother and I would be invited to 'tour' with him on weekends. Invariably, the car would break down, and my father leap out from behind the wheel and kick the tires in an effort to get it started again. These demonstrations of speechless rage foreshadowed his responses to the challenges of golf.

I was never told how or when my father discovered golf. I was about fourteen years old when it happened. He responded to this manifestation in the way that Balboa may have reacted when he found the Pacific Ocean from high upon a peak in Darien: jubilantly. The country club my father joined so that he might learn to excel at golf was operated by the proprietors of the most successful speakeasy in New York during the years of Prohibition, the '21' Club, also known as Jack & Charley's.

My father prepared carefully for his introduction to golf. He had two contrasting sets of bespoke 'plus-sixes' tailored by Edward J. Dillon. He acquired properly cleated shoes from Abercrombie & Fitch, and a golf bag filled with sticks: irons properly numbered, spoons, brassies; two putters and two golf balls as a precaution against the unlikely case that one would be lost. He corresponded with Dr James Nolan, the St Andrews-based collector-dealer of antique golf sticks, and one of the teachers, Henry Ketcham, of the philosophy of golf. My father joined the New York Athletic

Club and the Downtown Athletic Club with the expectation that he could get himself invited to become a member of their Golf Committees and, by association, have revealed to himself all the secrets of the grand old game.

It would be fruitless to try to evaluate the cost of all these necessities because it would have to be estimated in 1929 dollars and therefore could not seem to come to much compared to their relative cost today. In all events the cost was, in the end, rackingly emotional, as my father tried so gallantly and fruitlessly to push a flyspeck with his nose up the awe-inspiring, glass-walled mountain called golf.

By this time my father had acquired his third successive automobile, a Dodge, a reliable car which seldom broke down, reducing the need for solutions from my father's shoes. We were all down in front of the apartment house, my mother, my small brother and I, to see him off to his first day of play. He was gaily confident when the car pulled away from us. He was more or less a broken man when he returned after darkness had fallen that evening.

'They think I am going to have to put myself in the hands of a professional,' I heard him tell my mother. It sounded bad, the way he told it, as if he was going to have to face brain surgery.

The next two years were terrible periods to remember. His regular companion, an equable man with whom he had served in the US Navy in World War I and a good friend, was an eye-witness to what happened every weekend, winters excepted. This man kept a diary, intending to record the events of those terrible days until the oppression of memory forbade him to carry on after the second weekend of golf with my father. The diary tells of my father's dramatic adventures in sand traps, water hazards and dog-legs. The friend told my mother that he had stopped keeping the diary 'for the good of golf'.

On a half-dozen occasions during our summer holidays from school, my brother and I were forced to ride with our parents to the distant country club to experience a reflection of the tyrannies my father was suffering in the name of golf.

We would be gathered on a terrace near the first tee. My father

and his companion would arrive from the clubhouse. The companion would drive the ball smartly far down the fairway, straight
and true, well up toward the green. My father would address the
ball, waggle his bottom, flap his elbows, go into his backswing,
then, his eyes fixed on the ball, he would arc the clubhead in a
perfect rotation, executing a textbook follow-through, and the ball
would fly off to either direction, at right angles to the tee.

My father had been at war, at sea, in a community of rough
and tough tars, but it does not seem possible that any of them
could have been able to bring themselves to articulate the very
nearly hysterical violence of the language my father would pro-
nounce after each attempted shot. The owners of the country club
were, after all, men whose main commerce had been with boot-
leggers, hijackers and mobsters whose knowledge of coarse language could have been far more shameful than colorful. Yet they
blanched at the words and at the volume of the sound of the words
my father used after each unavailing drive.

It was revealed that he had, along the way of four months' time,
accumulated quite a store of reserve golf balls, proving that a
supply of two is inadequate to round out a golf game. In the few
dozen times I watched my father attempt, at the first tee, to drive
one of these toward a putting green he would need to use up not
less than six balls before he succeeded in putting one (more or
less) straight down the fairway.

Each Saturday and Sunday evening my brother and I, ears to a
door, would hear my mother pleading with my father to give up
golf. She would have far better used her persuasion by trying to
get Roddy McDowell to give up Lassie. My father was a self-made
man. He had put himself through law school, he had risen in
the navy, he had achieved life-of-the-party status entirely by the
application of his will. What was golf, as a relative value/challenge,
compared to those other mountains he had conquered?

My father was always calm in these discussions with my mother.
As the months wore on he became calmer and calmer as he seemed
to listen to my mother's urgent messages; but he couldn't have
been listening at all. Instead the house began to fill with books
which explained, one after another, almost diametrically opposite

JOE 'BANANAS' POZZO
CAPTAIN 1927

BIG AL,
CAPTAIN 1928

EDDIE CREMATORIO
CAPTAIN 1929

BUTCH O'RIELLY
CAPTAIN 1911

MACHINEGUN KELLY
CAPTAIN 1930

TONI 'THE CREEP' BRILLO
CAPTAIN 1931

WILD DOG TRIMBLE
CAPTAIN 1932

BUGSY NEW
CAPTAIN

ways to achieve conflicting golfing methods and techniques. Until late at night, in the main room of our apartment, he would teach himself all of the myriad ways of gripping golf sticks, working from odd diagrams and photographs, each one antithetical to the other.

He switched from plus-sixes to slacks and, for a while, this seemed to drop his golf score from 137 to 133 for eighteen holes, his best scores ever, but still well under championship play. Every night at home he would putt golf balls across the carpet toward an open-mouth tumbler. 'Toward', not 'into', is the correct usage here.

The old-time propensity to kick a car's tires now took the costly form of breaking golf sticks suddenly across his knee, or flinging them in random directions across the fairways and putting greens to the point where the Executive Committee had him in to closed sessions eleven times on charges made by the Greens Committee.

Then, out of the blue and to the dismay of our entire family, most certainly including my father, he developed a disfiguring rash upon his hands. He was forced to wear gloves all day, whether trying cases in court or facing clients across his desk. He was sent by our family doctor, a sadly puzzled man at best, to a dermatologist. Salves and ointments were prescribed and applied. His friend and fellow golfer had to undertake to drive the car to the country club and back twice each weekend because my father's hands were too slippery to hold the wheel.

The medications did not eliminate the rash, which had become a pitiable sight, unresponsive to the healer's art, far more eruptive than, say, leprosy, until the desperate dermatologist recommended – demanded – that my father consult a psychologist.

The psychologist solved the riddle. The cause of the heinous rash he said, was golf itself. It was not, he explained, that my father's hands were allergic to the leather bindings on the handles of golf sticks. He looked my father directly in the eye, according to my mother, who sat beside him through this worst ordeal, the first defeat, of his life. Golf itself had caused the trauma which, if allowed to continue, would spread across my father's body until he would appear so repellent that no caddy would go near him.

My father's character changed after that. He became a light-hearted, almost happy-go-lucky man who didn't seem to care a damn whether other people were capable of equalling his perform-ance as a human on any level. The two or three hundred people directly involved in the tragedy – his fellow golfers, comically relieved caddies, waiters and greenkeepers, our entire family – all experienced that sense of salvation which enthralls a born-again Christian. But within this same miracle which had come to pass, the revelation of revelations was that my father seemed thrilled and grateful that he would no longer need to make that long journey and back twice a week in order to demonstrate to the world that he couldn't play golf.

He was made well again, but the awful gift of golfing ineptitude passed out of my father's karma and into mine. From the day he retired from the grand, old game until this day, I have never been able to hit a golf ball.

Private Gallery

Bill Deedes

A lifetime of playing and watching golf, if you think about it, stores an enormous picture gallery in the mind. Most of the pictures, moreover, are of scenes and episodes on golf courses we are happy to remember. The humiliating episodes, mercifully, are left out: human nature being what it is, the mind is wonderfully selective.

My own gallery, in the hands of an exceptionally benevolent director, is open all 24 hours of the day. This means I am at liberty to stroll round it whenever my mind is idle. It is a haven from bores, a welcome relief to speeches which go on too long, a breath of fresh air when the smoke-filled room is full of men arguing interminably with each other, of inestimable comfort when the train in which you are travelling is running over an hour late.

There are risks attached to a tour of my gallery. A voice suddenly breaks out of the hum of argument, from which one has long passively withdrawn. 'Bill, do you have any view on this?' Thus summoned from the haze of the first tee at Sunningdale on an early summer's day promising great heat later on, it is necessary to think quickly. 'No STRONG view', I reply. This is usually well-received by people who still have a lot more to say.

My pictures are not hung in any particular order, but at the entry to the gallery is an unfading portrait of Bobby Jones at Royal St George's in 1930. It was his finest year, unlikely to be excelled. It was the year he took the highest amateur and professional honours here and in the United States. A local friend of my father offered to motor me over to St George's which was not many miles from our home in East Kent and where the Walker Cup was being played.

The gallery was small, including I remember Lady Astor and Douglas Fairbanks Senr. I was at liberty to wander more or less where I liked with my Brownie camera. Indeed, Bobby Jones stopped on his way to the tee to offer me a snap I still possess. He was not under pressure, but was inflicting a severe defeat on Roger Wethered. I see him clearly now, in my gallery, in grey flannel plus fours, blue stockings and matching pullover and a white cap. I see even more clearly that wonderfully unhurried swing which entered him in a class apart.

Half a century later, when the Open came to St George's, I recalled in a speech this earlier encounter, adding that I had in my pocket one of the old snaps to prove it. Tom Watson, who came so close to winning the Masters at Augusta in 1991, was at the dinner. He came up afterwards, asked to see the snap of Jones, examined it closely and handed it back to me. 'You were lucky,' someone said later, 'he's an ardent collector.' Until the Second World War I could keep my memory of Bobby Jones alive with one of those little flicker books, which illustrated his swing. Alas, it went with much else in the war.

Another pre-war memory, which offers comic relief in my gallery, was a round of golf with Sir Philip Sassoon, then Member of Parliament for Hythe and Folkestone, and Minister of Works. We met and became friendly at the House of Commons because I was for a time the *Morning Post*'s political correspondent. On the appointed day I arrived punctually at the Hythe golf course to find Sir Philip lined up with four caddies.

Two of these, he explained, would carry our clubs. Two would go forward and spot where our respective shots finished. This precaution would eliminate the time wasted in looking for golf balls. By this means we scorched our way round the course in not much over two hours. Who won was immaterial. We were both engaged in beating the clock. As we finished, Sir Philip paid off the caddies, jumped into his open car, which the chauffeur had brought as close as he could to the 18th green, invited me to join him, and we drove at speed to his private beach hut some five miles away.

A rapid swim and he was out of the water, back in his car and away, calling to me that a second car would arrive when I was ready to race me back to Port Lympne, his home in Kent, for lunch. The first person I met there was Sassoon's cousin, an astute woman who well understood his funny ways. 'What have you been doing to Philip?' she exclaimed. 'He says he is exhausted, and is resting in bed before lunch.' Anyone, with or without four caddies, who tries to get round a hilly golf course in just over two hours needs a rest before lunch.

By contrast I once spent six hours playing a round of golf in Mobile, Alabama. Three local bankers had volunteered to entertain me, a waif engaged in an unremunerative Foreign Office lecture tour. It was a hot day. We halted for refreshment at a Cola stand every third hole. The bankers had a lot of business to discuss. Furthermore, so complex was the scoring in our golf game that time was needed periodically to check the calculations.

I was on an allowance of only $25 a day from the Foreign Office and had twinges of anxiety about the progress of the game. It was a relief when my partner entered the locker room after the game, carrying a fistful of dollar bills and coins, which he declared to be my share of the winnings. They represented about three days' subsistence.

Apart from this singular experience, the best of my pictures in this small wing of the gallery relate to winning small sums in unusual circumstances. Many years ago E. W. Swanton, doyen of the cricket writers, and I found ourselves confronted by Ian Fleming and partner in a golf game at Royal St George's. 'Anything on the game?' someone asked casually as we left the first tee. 'Why not the usual?' said Fleming. We strolled on.

'What is the usual, by the way?' asked Swanton cautiously on the next tee. 'Hundred?' said Fleming. This was around 1964, so we were talking of about £400 in today's money. 'Why not a golf ball?' said Swanton, with the thoughtful air of a man unveiling a novelty. 'By all means,' said Fleming, who seemed intrigued by such an original proposal. In the end Swanton and I won the match. It by no means follows that we would have won £100.

I have another picture of Sunningdale Old Course a few years back, where the Parliamentary Golfing Society were playing a match. My partner for the afternoon round was Denis Thatcher. As we took our seats for lunch, I looked round for Denis, who was missing. Then a Sunningdale member sat down, nodded confidently to his partner for the afternoon and murmured smugly, 'He's well into his second gin.' I smelt a rat, or rather a plot on foot to stitch us up.

After lunch, I murmured my suspicions to Denis Thatcher. He matched my determined look. Things went well for us. After four or five holes, we were comfortably ahead. Our opponents signified their intention to write off their loss and embark on a new match. We agreed, and maintained our lead. Before we finished, we had embarked on a third match, which we also won. The fruits of victory were modest, properly so: but the victory itself was exceptionally sweet.

Another wing of my gallery carries portraits of golf courses overseas, where golf had usually to be stolen from other duties and carried the delicious whiff of truancy. In 1990, I undertook a rapid tour of three countries in South America. It never crossed my mind that those responsible for my arrangements would find a corner for golf. Yet in Brasilia, the British Ambassador found the corner of a Wednesday afternoon which enabled me to play 18 holes on the solitary golf course of that new capital. When I reached Chile, they said that Sunday afternoon would be wasted unless I found it convenient to play golf. In Lima, capital of Peru, there was just time for 9 holes between a luncheon and an early evening engagement.

None of these outings were really stolen, because my hosts insisted that there was nothing usefully to be done at the time except to play golf. It crossed my mind that they positively welcomed a guest who required them as an act of duty to visit a golf course. The fact is that the Englishman working overseas arranges his recreation more sensibly than we do here. The chances are that he is working in his office before 7 a.m. In the course of what might otherwise be a 15-hour day, he sets aside a couple or three hours for physical recreation.

It is the London commuter, who condemns himself to travelling a couple of hours to his work and back, who leads the unnatural life. The ambassador who plays two rounds of golf every week is not wasting Her Majesty's time. He is making sensible use of his own time, and benefiting his health.

All this is easier in cities where golf courses are only a few minutes' drive away. In days when I regularly visited Rhodesia, now Zimbabwe, usually for not more than three days at a time, we could reckon that the Royal Salisbury Golf Course was not more than ten minutes' drive from Meikle's Hotel in the centre of Salisbury. Sydney in Australia has a string of golf courses closer to the heart of the city than any of London's.

Melbourne is a sprawling city, but one can drive to the Royal Melbourne Golf Course in less time than it takes to reach Hampstead from the City. New Delhi has a golf course near the heart, where I once had a disastrous round with Sir George Sinclair, British administrator and later Member of Parliament for Dorking, when we were in India with a parliamentary select committee. It was disastrous because our caddies tipped off their friends who worked ahead, pocketed our golf balls, and then, through the agency of our caddies, offered to sell them back to us. This reduces a competitive game to farce.

It is some years since I played in Singapore. But in the old days there was a 9-hole course attached to the Government Guest House – on which Lee Kuan Yew played regularly. By a wonderful stroke of luck the professional at my home course, Cyril Horne, moved to Singapore in search of fame and fortune. Thereafter whenever I passed through the island, we contrived to play a few holes together and he would mark the occasion with one or two gifts from his shop.

Thus, when visiting golf clubs which consider themselves in the upper echelon, I sometimes put on the faded tie of the Royal Singapore Golf Course – which I have played, but to which I have never belonged. Every now and again one gets a nibble. Some senior figure who served the Empire when the sun never set on it, peers at my tie and exclaims incredulously, 'You were a member of the Royal Singapore?' I make light of it. He is impressed.

Cyril Horne had enormous charisma and when the time came for the British to wind up their military bases and leave the island, he settled down to the task of enabling the Chinese to enjoy golf on what had been virtually exclusive British property. I have a happy picture in my mind of Cyril on the vast practice ground working with a contingent of Chinese learners, playfully whacking their backsides with the shaft of a club and shouting expletives at them. He won our hearts.

When Lord Selkirk was our Commissioner for Singapore, he recommended Horne for a modest honour, on grounds that his contribution to cementing race relations in Singapore had been outstanding. Nothing came of it, but Horne at least had the satisfaction of getting Lee Kuan Yew's handicap down to the edge of single figures.

Golf almost anywhere in South Africa is a delight, but particularly on courses round Johannesburg, where the elevation and slightly rarer atmosphere makes the ball fly further. There is a macabre picture in my gallery of a round of golf in Johannesburg. It was a hot day. My partner and I were playing two members of the club who had generously offered to be our hosts.

It was one of those golf clubs where members were required to record their score at every hole on a card, and to enter this card into the club's computer for reassessment of handicap immediately on return to the club house. On the final holes my mind began to turn to a pint of beer in the club house. It would, I reckoned, go down without touching the sides. Forgive us, said our hosts as we limped on to the club's terrace, if we first sort out these cards. Their calculations were prolonged, because under club rules double and triple bogeys had to be converted into something lower. As we waited, my thirst became a danger to my health.

By contrast, there are several pictures in my overseas gallery of golf at Johannesburg's River Club, founded many years ago by 'Punch' Barlow of Barlow Rand. He established the sound tradition by which who wins and how the card reads takes second place to hospitality. Early morning starters can break off at an early hole and take a light breakfast under the trees.

Nearer home, I have in my mind's eye the sort of picture Sir John Lavery might have painted of Newcastle, Co. Down, where the mountains of Mourne go down to the sea. Lavery comes to mind because some of his pictures hang in the hall of Stormont Castle. After an anniversary dinner in Belfast, my hosts suggested a visit to Newcastle. What lingers in my mind, as well as the mountains and the delights of this golf course, is the warmth with which we were received in the club house. For years now, we have neglected the great golf courses of Ulster and the Republic, foolishly supposing that to play there is dangerous. In reality, it is safe as houses and the warmth of welcome touching.

I made my own introduction to Scottish golf years ago when, if they were desperately short of a political speaker, the Unionist office in Glasgow or Edinburgh called on me. An agent up there was a keen golfer, and I put it to her that a speech would always be forthcoming in return for a round of golf. That proved a most satisfactory arrangement, at least for me.

There was one memorable week-end when a parliamentary colleague, Gil Leburn, then a Scottish Under Secretary, wanted to persuade me to address a fete in his constituency, Kinross and West Perthshire, on August Bank Holiday Monday. There was an exceptionally high price to be exacted for that favour. We will, he said, travel up on Friday evening by sleeper and play the Old Course at St Andrews on Saturday. On Sunday we will play Kings and Queens at Gleneagles. On Monday we will go to the fete, and return you to England, home and beauty on the night sleeper. Alas, my generous host died, absurdly young, on a fishing trip soon after.

One thing I have learned in my life: there are not enough days in which to play more than a fraction of this country's great golf courses, so an opportunity should never be neglected. Some years back, I was invited by the Press Golfing Society to be their president. By long tradition, the president's day is held at Walton Heath. He gives the prizes. On the first of these occasions, the secretary and I met for lunch to discuss arrangements.

When we had agreed on the sum needed for the prizes, I was moved to ask, 'By the way, am I allowed to play?' He looked astonished. Then he went on to point out that not all past presidents (usually newspaper proprietors) had even attended the prizegiving. They bought the prizes and that was that. I made it plain that to travel to Walton Heath late in the evening in order to give away my prizes held few attractions. I have played on this particular day every year since. In the year I won one of my own prizes, I settled for a bottle of champagne.

Those of us who play for the Parliamentary Golfing Society – which marked its centenary in 1991 – are more fortunate than we deserve or perhaps realise. Since days when Lady Astor manoeuvred her way into the final of the Parliamentary Golf Handicap to play against the Prince of Wales, the Society has spread its wings. It receives invitations to play matches on great courses, Huntercombe, Sunningdale, Walton Heath, Woking, Royal St George's, the Berkshire among them, culminating in a short late-summer tour which embraces one outstanding course in the North of England and one in Scotland – usually Muirfield, Prestwick, or St Andrews.

Golf with the Society's President, Lord Whitelaw, has produced many joyful pictures for the mind's album. We were once partners in the Parliamentary Handicap, which was then played at Royal Mid-Surrey. As we approached the first tee, the rain set in. We handed over our cards and umbrellas to Whitelaw's two minders, begged them to keep our respective (Stableford) scores and reconciled ourselves to a soaking. At the end of our round they produced two sodden golf cards on which it was just possible to decipher, 'Whitelaw 34, Deedes 33.' 'There's loyalty for you!' I exclaimed.

Then there was the strange episode of the caddy at Prestwick when the Society were playing against the club. 'How old might Lord Whitelaw be?' one of them asked me during our morning round. His match was just behind our own. 'Born in 1918,' I said confidently, having heard him say so the night before. The elderly caddy shook his head maddeningly and was supported by his mates. One of them, who caddied for Lord Whitelaw (a member of Prestwick for 40 years), insisted that he was nearer 80.

'Absurd,' I said. 'He is younger than I am.' The caddies smiled and winked with maddening superiority. During the lunch hour I warned the Lord President of the Council, as he then was, of this absurd confusion. After the lunch interval, Whitelaw approached the first tee belligerently and before the assembled caddies made a public statement about his age. The old caddy refused to budge an inch, wagged his head and moved off, leaving Lord Whitelaw dumbfounded. In desperation at the end of the afternoon, he produced his driving licence as a trump card. The caddies would have none of it, pointing out that the first two digits on the licence were 1 and 0. 'Born in 1910, like we said,' they declared. It will be sad when golf finally loses caddies of such obstinate character.

All sport carries pictures in the mind; but for all seasons, in all weathers and now in almost every country in the world, golf's gallery is wonderfully rich. I never tire of walking round the corridors of mine. There is no charge: and in a country so devoted to committee meetings which go on far too long, it is indispensable.

OBSESSION

Martin Johnson

You can be black or white, introvert or extrovert, male or female, but to my mind there are only two types of people in the world: golfers and non-golfers. Once bitten, it is akin to having your neck punctured in Transylvania – there is no known antidote. If the Prince of Darkness offered to turn a swing that resembles a man attempting to chop wood inside a telephone kiosk into a thing of awesome power and beauty, I think I would have to sign up and take my chance with the afterlife.

I might watch cricket for a living, but it would have to be a Test match of rare quality for me not to wish upon it a four-day finish in order to squeeze in an extra round of golf. When England were playing the West Indies at Lord's a couple of summers ago, and other members of the Press Box had their heads buried inside a *Wisden Almanac*, the *Guardian* correspondent and I spent the entire day demonstrating the respective merits of the Vardon grip and the interlocking method on the rubber aerial of his portable phone.

We are, by and large, inseparable on overseas cricket tours, in that, to us, a Test match against India means not so much the thought of being enchanted by turbaned purveyors of wristy flight and spin as the prospect of a round or two at Royal Delhi. There is a certain amount of danger involved, including the kamikaze tendencies of the auto-rickshaw drivers charged with getting you there, a sliced drive into cobra country, and the ever-present threat of being decapitated by a flying clubhead from hire-sets dating back to well before the first days of the Raj. However, golf in foreign parts has a charm all of its own.

During the 1987 tour to Pakistan we had a game in Peshawar, which is not much more than a three wood from the Khyber Pass, and were greeted by the usual avalanche of volunteer caddies when we drove in. There are not many qualifications for being a caddy on the sub-continent: you have to be barefoot, and either have to be eight years old or eighty. I got one of the latter, who took me on to the first tee and handed me a driver. 'No, no, iron for safety,' I said, plucking out a three, and dunked the ball straight into swamp about fifty yards ahead. Off towards the hazard I trudged, held out my hand for another ball, but my caddy had disappeared. A minute or so elapsed, whereupon a strange gurgling noise came from the foul expanse of water, and a wizened hand arose like Excalibur from the lake clutching a ball. 'Bloody hell,' I said. 'What a caddy.' Fixing me with a grin that was entirely toothless, my man emerged from the swamp. 'You very lucky, sir. In snake season, I no dive. We lose two caddies last year.'

During the course of the round, I remained a very lucky golfer, as indeed did my opponent. Every time one of our balls disappeared into the trees, so did the caddy, and there – miraculously – was the ball, sitting up on an anthill as though on a tee-peg, on the only clear route to the green. With one of these boys to carry your bag, you can go round in even par without ever hitting a decent shot.

On one occasion at Royal Delhi, the then *Times* correspondent was one of our opponents in a fourball. Not the longest of hitters, he instructed his caddy at a par three to 'hand me my one-wood' and scuffed the ball all along the ground towards a hidden green. Off we strode, and were suddenly regaled by a great roar from the forecaddies away in the distance. 'Hole in one, sir!' he was told when we reached the green – which, as club tradition would have it, meant a substantial reward in the rupee department for all bag-carriers and spotters. To this day he wonders whether his first hole in one was entirely genuine. No one in our group had ever holed in one, although I do hold the curious distinction – via an inglorious shank and a ricochet off a startled golfer in the process of putting out – of a hole in one on the wrong green.

As it happens, *The Times* managed to recover most of the money on one of the more novel forms of side bet that accompanies any game involving the then BBC and now *Daily Telegraph* cricket correspondent. He is one of those rare individuals who does not swear, but is unfortunate enough to have a golf game that demands some kind of emotional release, and he gets round this problem by exchanging the names of musical composers for oaths whenever he hits a bad shot. 'Schubert!' is comparatively mild, more or less equating to 'bother', 'Brahms!' and 'Beethoven!' come into a more serious category, while a complete duff carries the ultimate in self-beratement, a 'Mendelssohn!' *The Times* won the side bet that day, struck before we went out, by correctly forecasting a Brahms round, which was clinched – by a short head from Beethoven – with a clatter into the trees at the 18th.

Thanks to cricket, I have played golf on some spectacular courses (Ballmecuan on New Zealand's South Island can scarcely be equalled for scenery), not to mention some bizarre ones, such as the one in Georgetown, Guyana. Times are hard in this run-down former British Colony, and if it was not for the architecture you would imagine that the clubhouse was the groundsman's hut. There is, in fact, no groundsman at all. The course is kept in trim by vast herds of goats and sheep, some of which end up in a cooking pot after wayward shots, and the three dozen or so club members take it in turns to hand-mow the greens. At the 19th you can get a warm beer – the cooler packed up in circa 1970 – and there is one dartboard and one dart. When we had a game on it after playing a round during England's 1990 tour to the West Indies, the dartboard fell off its nail, and a large bat – snoozing quietly behind the bullseye – flew out. The Press Association correspondent, in the process of throwing, was so startled that his dart shot sideways like a fast socket, perforated one of the ceiling fans, and dislodged several green lizards.

Playing on a desert course, as we did in Dubai when England were involved in a one-day tournament in nearby Sharjah, is something different, not so much for the oil- and mud-compacted greens, or browns, as for the fact that every shot is off sand. The reward for hitting the fairway, identifiable only by marker posts, is to play your next shot off a synthetic 'grass' tee carried around

with you, and the only difference in being in a 'bunker', as opposed
to the rough, is that you cannot ground your club. It is a matter
of some regret to me that England, as yet, have no plans for a Test
match in the Sudan, where there is apparently a course consisting
of nine holes but only one flag. It is not made of wood, because
the ants would look upon it as breakfast, but metal, and as this
would by all accounts quickly be pinched by the locals and melted
down, a boy is permanently employed to rush it from hole to hole.

A bit closer to home, golf in Ireland is one of life's great pleasures, although given that it is overrun with Americans in the
summer season, it is high time that the Irish Golf Association
declared cigar butts to be loose impediments rather than obstruc-
tions. The fairways in July and August are knee deep in the things.
It was in Ireland, asking for directions for a trip from LaHinch to
Waterville, that we actually received the apocryphal Irish reply of:
'I wouldn't start from here if I were you.' My colleague from *The
Guardian*, though, has a better story, which he swears is true: he
and a friend ordered a 7 a.m. alarm call to get them up for an
early morning round. He woke, as it happened, a touch earlier,
and was having a shave when he heard a noise at the door and
turned round to see a note being shoved underneath. 'Please call
the switchboard at 7 a.m.', it read. This he did, and a voice
answered: 'Very sorry, sir, but there's something wrong with the
system and we can't make outward calls to the rooms. So this is
your early morning reminder.'

Golf in this country is not quite so bizarre, more's the pity, but
it has given me just as much pleasure – especially when I had a
less anti-social job, with things like summer holidays, and went
away in a foursome for golf, cards and four or five days of late
night drinking and early morning rising. The latter combination
made for some interesting scenes around the first tee, and there
was one particularly embarrassing moment at a club in Norfolk.
The four of us arrived, in various stages of disrepair, and were
early enough to head a sizeable queue of immaculately turned
out golfers, most of them being, one would have guessed, retired
admirals and magistrates. The first tee shot, mine, just hobbled
past the ladies' tee, and turned out to be comfortably the best of

the four. The next scuttled off the toe on to the practice putting green, the next was sliced out of bounds, and the last flew off the heel, down some steps, through a pair of patio doors, and finished underneath a snooker table. The best we could do was make some feeble joke about needing a collar and tie to go in and play it, but as silences go, I have never experienced a stonier one.

The toe-ended scuttle belonged to the one amongst us known as Nobby, who was not quite so passionate about the game as the rest of us. He had, I recall, an extraordinary wooden club with a black head which he referred to as the 'mamba'. It had, resulting from a fit of temper some years previously, a bizarrely twisted head, which made it produce the same kind of high slice whether played off tee-peg, fairway, or, as it often was, for soft delicate shots out of a bunker. Nobby enjoyed his golf, even though a propensity to shank occasionally resulted in him covering 360 degrees and arriving back, seven or eight shots later, at the precise spot he started from. He did, however, enjoy a pint substantially more, and even though he once struck such a purple patch that he reached the semi-final of the Sunday morning knockout organised by the Leicester *Mercury* (the newspaper we all worked for), he conceded his match when two up with three to play because the pub was open.

Another of our four was Charlie, who would have been a fairly decent golfer had the game not involved the art of putting. Like so many before him, he developed the yips, and watching him from three feet or so was like watching a man attempting to hole out with an electric eel. It has afflicted more celebrated golfers than Charlie down the years, including Harry Vardon, and I rather like the story of Vardon being approached by a lady convinced that drink was the root of his problems, and urging him to sign the pledge. 'Madam,' he is alleged to have responded, 'I have lost many matches in my career, but never, never in my life, have I lost one to a teetotaller.' There is probably a form of the yips in most sports. Certainly there is in cricket, where it appears, rather unkindly, to home in on left-arm spinners. The worst case I have seen was that of the Derbyshire bowler Fred Swarbrook, who could bowl high full tosses, low scuttlers, or deliveries that failed to leave the hand at all with equal facility. He finally gave up after bowling one ball that he lost all sight of. As he stood in the bowler's crease frantically scanning the radar, down it came from the vertical and hit him on top of the head.

The fourth member of our group, Robin, was a truly awful player. We went up, just the two of us, to play a few rounds in Scotland one summer, and came to the first tee in Carnoustie where we were offered – but declined – the services of one of a large gathering of sage and wizened Scottish caddies. Robin teed off, spanked it down the middle, much to his amazement, and received generous applause from the locals. Four hours and, at a rough estimate, 150 blows later, he hit a four iron from the 18th fairway next to the pin, and was applauded in by the same group, who presumably thought he had shot a 66. A couple of years later, he flew off his motorbike, and his journey towards a hedge was only interrupted by a lamppost being in the way of his right elbow. He left hospital with a permanently bent arm, but in terms of his golf, a miracle had been performed. He discovered, despite an elbow that resembles a chicane on a motor racing track, that he could now do nothing but hit the ball gun-barrel straight. He played very well for several years, before giving up golf for sailing, which suggested to me that his head must have made contact with the lamppost as well as his elbow.

It is difficult to imagine life without golf, even though it now costs me large amounts of money. From a single-figure handicap based around a controlled draw, I now hack around with an uncontrollable slice, but my one concession to this is in giving up a particularly bottom-clenching form of golf known as Las Vegas. It involves a fourball better ball, in which the two scores from one partnership are placed side by side to form a number. Ergo, two par fours will give your team 44. The opposition might have a four and a five (45), in which case the lower figure is subtracted – leaving 1 – and if, say, you are playing 10p per point, you will leave the first green 10p ahead.

However, if neither member of a partnership acquires par, the higher figure is placed first. Ergo, a nine and a five will make 95, and when 44 is taken away from that, you are walking off the first

green £5.10 behind. Even worse, should the opposition make a birdie (34) then they have the right to double your score. Ninety-five becomes 190, minus 34 equals 156. You are now £15.60 down. The first time I played this game was about 20 years ago, when I was earning £30 per week, and without knowing it holed a putt that saved our team £7.50. Delayed shock set in, as it did when something similar happened to a friend of mine when he was asked to make up a four one Sunday morning at the club he had just joined. 'We play for a wrapped ball,' said one of the other three, in the days when new golf balls came in a paper wrapper. 'That okay by you?' 'Fine,' said my friend, and he duly went on to win a match that one of the other three appeared to have in his pocket by holing out from a bunker at the 18th. They shook hands and repaired to the 19th, where he was presented with three brand-new golf balls all wrapped with a £50 note. There was some consternation when he promptly fainted.

My brother, who lives in Belgium, plays every Boxing Day morning in a match in which fainting at the end of the round is less common than passing out before you have even struck off the first tee. Handicaps are noted, at which point you are then given one hour in which – under scrutiny – to drink as many bottles of beer as you can in that time in exchange for one extra stroke per beer. Thereby, a scratch golfer who is also a scratch drinker can find himself playing off 10 or 11. The secret, according to my brother, who has won this event several times, is to play for the middle one of the three balls you can see when your hour's drinking is up.

For most of us, however, the game is hard enough when stone cold sober. Non-golfers cannot understand what a humbler the game is, and how, say, Margaret Thatcher would have been a good bit less haughty had she ever had the experience of topping and duffing her way to a 10 and 8 thrashing in a Ladies' single. It is, perhaps, the easiest game in the world for making you look a complete prat, which, in a perverse sort of way, is why I am totally addicted to it.

AN INVITATION TO GOLF

George V. Higgins

A generous and hospitable (but not completely trustworthy) friend, having purchased a condominium with a splendid southerly view of the Atlantic and a northerly view of a private championship golf course, invited my wife and me for a long-weekend visit. Unprepared for the invitation, but aware of his perplexing habit of devoting leisure time to golf's mysterious rituals, I surmised he had in mind not three decorous days of sun-bathing, reading, and ocean-gazing (perhaps with a beverage or two) on the sundeck, but what some sage called a good walk spoiled. I played for time and more data. 'We don't have clubs,' I said.

'We have two extra sets,' he said, with the little smile of chop-licking anticipation that the cat exhibits over a bird it's pounced upon and disabled. 'The Wilson Staff Professionals we bought two years ago. We gave each other new Pings for Christmas.' So I *had* known what he was up to.

'I didn't make myself clear,' I said. 'We don't have clubs because we don't commit golf. We take the same attitude toward golf that we take toward exotic sexual practices. We don't think the state should try to regulate either one. So long as golf's done privately by consenting adults, and we're not expected to participate, it's perfectly all right with us.'

'But I've *seen* you play golf,' he said, with the same chagrined expression that the cat displays when the bird unexpectedly recovers its senses, ascertains its injuries are superficial, and as the cat too long dawdles smugly preparing for the kill, escapes into the air. 'I saw you play golf in college.' Which of course was his motive for trying to lure me on to his golf course: confident he knew who would relish the ecstasy of victory, and who was destined to suffer the agony of defeat. He may even have had betting in mind. My friend has a little mean streak.

'No, you didn't,' I said with firmness. 'You are mistaken, my friend.'

Brought up as I was (most happily, otherwise) by forebears passionately and irrationally devoted to the fortunes (mostly ill, since 1918) of the Boston Red Sox, as an apprentice male I uncritically assumed: firstly, that in spring, in New England, a young man's fancy rightly ought to turn to baseball, and secondly that he would surely be rewarded by success in the endeavor (said success perhaps headily even including the swooning admiration of young ladies, said to be somewhat addled by the sight of crocuses appearing from the mud).

In that general view, *I* was mistaken, not only in the major assumptions but in several others as well (the maidens did indeed swoon, but not into my arms, despite my calf-eyed hopes). To the benefit of my adult skills at resignation, I discovered that the game of baseball demands not only dedication (which I had in abundance, to the conversational distraction of my mother, who disliked the sport), and practice (to which I allocated many, many hours, to the neglect of my schoolwork and detriment of my general intellectual improvement), but also, sadly, ability. Ability I lacked.

Oh, my eyes were sharp enough, but not co-ordinated with my hands and feet. Or any of my other limbs, feeble as they were. The eyes perceived the task at hand; the brain efficiently registered the perception and instructed the pertinent muscles and stuff to respond appropriately. But while everything happened in due course, it invariably seemed to happen too late, and not at all as I'd had in mind. I realised, after more than a decade of contests followed by despair, that I Just Couldn't Play The Game. So I gave it up.

By then I was too old and, having lacked the good judgment to have been born rich, too poor, to take up polo; too light and too slow to play American football (too prudent as well; devil take the padding and the armored helmets: those mammoth bozos collide with each other at locomotive speed, *on purpose*); and by reason of normal height unqualified for basketball, even if that had been played in the summer, which it wasn't, then. Tennis? Forget it. Nobody played tennis in those days, except for the never-sweaty ladies who patty-caked the ball back and forth to while away the hours while their gentlemen played polo.

Still, I had to find something. It's so cold and so dreary in New England so much of the year that every thinking person yearns for some pleasant, non-exhausting, reasonably priced form of summer recreation. I began to scout around for one that wouldn't kill me, in wallet, body or spirit. Memory suggested a lead.

When I was growing up, Ted Williams played left field for the Boston Red Sox. Some have argued (I'm among them) that he achieved his ambition of becoming the greatest hitter who ever lived. Williams years before I gave up baseball had squelched Sam Snead's superior and mirthful claim that golf's more difficult than baseball by telling Sam he'd like to see him hit that damned thing straight if it were to be thrown at him at 90 mph, instead of being perched on a peg, sitting-duck still, a convenient inch off the ground. I had inadvertently seen Sam Snead on television. He was *old* (46, which in 1958 was practically elderly, but now's mere striplinghood), and appeared not to have skipped too many meals. I was 18, lithe and limber, compared to him. If Ted Williams said golf was easy, and that paunchy old bird was a champion – well, the deduction was obvious.

It was that I must be precisely the species of animal for whom golf had been invented. Scotsmen dreamed it up, right? The same lads who find it amusing to heave telephone poles around, use brooms to slide heavy discs along ice, and engage in shin-kicking contests? Eat sheep guts stuffed with oatmeal, washed down with whisky, neat? It had to be *the* pastime for the athletically hopeless, the terminally clumsy, in whose company I certainly belonged. I made enquiries among those seasoned at the game. None of them looked a bit like an athlete. All claimed to have been relaxed and refreshed by their outings. Precisely what I was after. I took up golf, and learned a lot from it.

Frustration's nature's milder way of getting our attention, so we'll educate ourselves. Golf surpassed frustration. It infuriated me. I had relatively little money to invest in equipment, so I had to accept right-hander's clubs; while I write with my right hand, and shoot and fish right-handed, it's only because my first instructors told me to do it that way, and back then I was meek. But I am also by a minuscule bit actually left-handed, and always throw with my left (albeit, alas, neither impressively far nor impressively fast). Still, no matter. Cheap equipment was as serviceable to my instruction as costlier clubs would have been. I learned:

– That on days when I could putt successfully I was quite unable to keep my drives out of the woods or my irons out of the bushes.

– That on days when I drove straight and true, and putted quite capably, I shanked all my iron shots. Into the woods again. If James Audubon had walked a few rounds with me, he would today be as renowned an arborist as he is an ornithologist. He would also be remembered for his proficiency at cursing and swearing, if he didn't master that art on his own.

– That on days when the irons and the putter were in good order, I launched virtually every tee-shot into the forest or the swamp. By doing so I discovered as well that while the symptoms of poison ivy, poison oak, and poison sumac are similar, those pernicious vegetations do not look the same – a keen eye for the recognition of poison ivy's no defense against the others. When you swing the head of your club through any such green plant (in order to splash the ball under it into the water-hazard 80 yards from the green), the metal shaft of the club collects toxic sap on the follow-through – it gets on your hands when you replace the club in the bag. Also discovered: that calamine lotion was not only not the panacea it had been cracked up to be; it wasn't even the effective palliative for which I gladly would have settled.

– That the reason people pay huge fees to join select private clubs is not necessarily religious or racial prejudice (although one of the two seems to have been the usual motive). It is because huge numbers of penurious and/or parsimonious persons resort to the public links, even during the week, so that it takes between seven and eight excruciating hours to play 18.

– That he who has a wicked slice/hook off the tee (I had both, invariably executing the one likely to cause the nastiest problem) is destined to spend a considerable sum on the purchase of new golf balls, not to mention the cost of the damage to his prospects of salvation resultant from the bad language employed on the occasion of each loss.

– That he who would really prefer to have a second cold lager, and then maybe a third and fourth, than to leave the clubhouse after the first cold beer, ritually taken at the turn to the back nine, should probably stay in the clubhouse and have the additional beer(s), thus sparing the other members of his foursome the agony of his antics, and himself the cardiac damage of the tantrums his misdeeds bring on.

– That I really don't like golf at all. When my then-wife, then-estranged, informed me with malicious satisfaction that she had cleaned out the basement of my then-house in my absence, and given my sticks away, I confounded her hopes by sincerely replying: 'Good. About time you did me a favor.' I did not respond as civilly when she disclosed she had sold my then-dog, a fairly stupid Dalmatian (if that is not a redundancy), but still a genuine dog, and a better diversion than golf.

I have, in other words, never played golf, just as I told my friend. 'But I saw you play golf,' he said plaintively. 'I was there. The same foursome. I saw you with my own eyes.'

'Think back on it,' I said. 'Remember what I did out there? Would you call that "playing golf"?'

'No,' he said after the moment it took the fact of defeat to sink in; 'no, I wouldn't at that.'

And neither would I. I raged at golf for a period of six or seven years, a quarter-century ago, and then one day adverted at last to the manifest fact that I loathed golf, and golf loathed me ('Funny game, golf.' 'Taint meant to be.') and I therefore should stop demeaning it while tormenting myself. I did. The only proper use of golf is on rainy winter Saturday afternoons: Turn on the devil box to some tournament under way in some faraway sunny clime and lie down on the couch to allow the announcers to whisper you off to your nap.

Naturally, having jettisoned golf as I had baseball, I was once again in the market for a summer sport which would not bankrupt me, kill me, or cause me to kill myself. But this time I was better fitted out. I had the advantages of maturity, good judgment, a keen grasp of reality. I found that perfect sport. I took up sailing (my friend uttered his long-weekend invitation during one of the eight summers when I was most unwillingly between my second and third boats, my teeth well-gnashed and heart filled with bitterness).

Sailing's a most restful time, or at least my version is. Since I own the boat (well, the bank has an interest), whatever I do is right, and whenever something goes wrong I get to bawl foul oaths at the crewman responsible. The skipper, you see, is never to blame; that is the law of the sea, and accounts not only for the placid demeanor and comfortable longevity of captains and admirals and such, but also for the bad end that Fletcher Christian met – and a good many modern divorces, too. You can trust the wind and the sea: either one will kill you if it gets half a chance (and if neither does, the bill from the boatyard will at least throw a good scare into you). You know where you stand, and I do – that's why I'm Captain Cautious, the Chicken of the Sea.

But that doesn't appease my good friend. When at last I got the third boat, I invited him and his wife to go sailing. I am also, you see, a generous and hospitable friend. He gazed at me with jaundiced eye. He knew what I was up to. He knew I knew he's afraid of the water, and cannot conceal his uneasiness, and that the only time he ever went out, he made such a sweaty fool of himself that everyone had to go back. 'Nothing doing,' he said. 'I don't do that. I know where I stand on sailing. I hate it. That's why I stand on the land.'

I didn't argue. After all, I generally knew where I stood, back in the days when I wasn't playing golf. I stood in the woods, or I stood in the rough, or I stood in a creek. Seldom did I find myself standing on the green, with a chance at par. The stubs in the checkbook tell me that small sloop in dollars isn't cheap at all, but in my heart I know there is nothing more expensive than that blasted game of golf.

For Amusement Only

Donald Trelford

Golf, as Henry Longhurst never tired of reminding us, is essentially a simple game. You just hit a ball with a stick towards a hole, 'overcoming as best you may such hazards as you encounter on the way'. I have never found it so and call on a lifetime's frustrations in support of the alternative view, articulated by Peter Dobereiner, that 'golf is a bastard'.

If it is really such a doddle, why – one has to ask – are the game's leading exponents esteemed higher than statesmen and rewarded like pop stars? As I ran out of balls last summer on a course near Marbella in Spain – having drowned *fourteen* of them in water – I came the closest I have ever done to giving up the game altogether. I didn't, of course, and I won't because one of golf's abiding addictions is the fact that you can't ever beat it.

No matter how good you may think you are, the game punishes those with the hubris to believe they've got it licked. I reckon something like that must have happened to Sandy Lyle at his peak, when he was widely quoted as saying that he expected to win a major every year. The golfing gods appeared to take that as an insult and his career went rapidly downhill from that point. Far from winning a major title every year, he may never win one ever again (though I live in hope of being proved wrong).

One of the explanations for the perennial genius of Jack Nicklaus, apart from his god-given talent and physique, is that he never takes the game for granted. As with women, once you do that you're finished. The game turns round and bites you. Nicklaus has never made that mistake. After a magical round of 63 in a US Open, he was asked how many of the strokes he had played that day he was happy with. 'Not one,' he replied briskly – 'but the score was OK.'

Not that over-confidence has ever been my problem. It isn't the golfing gods who direct my ball into trees and water – and, let's be completely honest, over the occasional passing road or club-house roof. I don't need Shakespeare to tell me that 'the fault, dear Brutus, lies not in our stars, but in ourselves, that we are thus and thus' – or, to be more precise, dear Brutus, the fault lies in our stance and grip and the fact that our backswing is much too fast.

I recently came across this portrait of my golfing style, written by my father-in-law, John Mark, for a family 'festschrift' on my fiftieth birthday:

To watch Donald on the first tee, addressing the ball, one is filled with a fearful fascination. That chunky figure, those powerful arms, that awesome determination – primeval forces are about to be unleashed. He is not just going to hit the ball – he is out to destroy it.

Mind you, with his right hand too far underneath the grip, he is bound to have an enormous slice and, believe me, he does, he does. The background music one hears in one's head is an old pop song, 'Something's Gonna Give, Something's Gonna Give, Something's Gonna Give'.

I once played Wentworth West Course with him in an *Observer* annual competition. You really have to be straight on that course, but most of the elaborate private gardens on the right of the fairways were peppered by Donald that morning. An awesome crack and yet another garden gnome laid a white, shiny, perfectly round egg.

The third member of the trio was a much better golfer than either of us. But then, he spent most of his life on golf courses and possessed one of the most expensive sets of clubs I have ever seen. In his spare time, he was an *Observer* printer. The whole round took 4½ hours, a lot of which was spent looking for balls.

The last game I had with Donald was on a nine-hole par three course, laid out by Tony Jacklin in Guernsey. While I was parking the car, typically Donald, he rushed off and paid the green fees – £10 for the two. When I protested, he eventually agreed to play the match for the £10.

We were standing 'All Square' on the ninth tee, about 180 yards. Donald had a good shot, nearly straight for him – about 20 yards to the right. I hit one dead straight but there was a stream across the front of the green with three stepping stones. To my horror the ball bounced once before the stream and then appeared to drop in on its second bounce. We walked down, and, after looking in the stream, found my ball about a foot from the hole. It had cleverly found the middle flat stepping-stone and gone straight on its merry way. Donald's demeanour and remarks could best be described as enigmatic.

Probably my most humiliating experience on a golf course – out of a great many blush-making episodes, I might add – was at Guadalmina in Spain, scene of that marvellous film, *A Touch of Class*, starring George Segal and Glenda Jackson. I had gone there for much the same reason they had, with golf on the side.

My holiday companion, now my wife, made the mistake of following me round the course one morning. As I hacked my way from bunker to tree to lake, she saw a side of my character she hadn't bargained for – and a range of language unknown at Cheltenham Ladies' College.

Finally, I ran out of golf balls. I was about to trail back grimly to the hotel, tail between legs, when a Spanish peasant emerged from the woods with a tray full of golf balls, going cheap. I seized them avidly and played on. It was only later that it dawned on me (and, to my chagrin, on Kate) that the balls I had paid for were my own. The old boy had clearly tracked me round the course, turning my misadventures to profitable account. I was reminded of the old golfing joke when a player says to his caddie: 'That was the worst round I've ever played.' To which the caddie replies: 'So you've played before then?'

One of my better moments on a golf course was on the

eighteenth green at Highgate, where, despite there being too many hilly bits for my taste, I still like to stagger round. I played my second shot with a seven-iron towards the green, which is uphill and slightly round the corner, right by the clubhouse and blind to the approaching player. I gave it a fair old whack, slightly off line to the right, and waited for the crash of a window in the clubhouse. There was an almighty crack all right, not unlike gunfire, but no sound of splintering glass.

Quelling a cowardly urge to leg it to the car-park and home, I wandered up warily towards the green. I couldn't help noticing as I did so that the clubhouse windows were full of faces, all peering up to locate the source of the alarming noise they'd heard. One or two people had gone outside and were looking around in a mystified fashion.

I then spotted my errant ball. It was about two inches from the flag. It had obviously rebounded off the clubhouse wall on to the green. So I was able to swagger up to it, ignoring the crowd, as if to say, 'Nothing to do with me, old beans.'

Standing on the tee is always a nightmare. I've read all the instruction books, I've had lessons, and it has done me no good at all. In some ways it has made things worse. I'm so conscious of where my head, my hands and my legs are stationed, of the fact that I must keep my arms straight and not swing too fast, that I'm all tensed up and almost paralytic. When I finally hit the ball – *if* I hit it – it seems a minor miracle of science and technology, nothing to do with sport.

I once paid ten dollars for a tennis lesson in Aspen, Colorado. After a few minutes' knock-up the pro said to me wearily: 'How long you been playing with that stumpy style?' 'About forty years,' I replied. 'In that case, take your ten dollars back. You don't want to start changing now.' I wish somebody had taken the same attitude to my golf.

I have a photograph of my father in plus-fours brandishing a mashie-niblick in 1930, the year Bobby Jones did the Grand Slam, and he is still playing twice a week in his eighties. Even so, he didn't introduce me to golf. That was the work of Des Wilson, now Chairman of the Liberal Democrats, who took me to play at

Sandown Park and Wimbledon Common when I was thirty-something.

I remember Des Wilson's advice to a beginner: 'First learn to hit the ball, then hit it straight, only then try to hit it a long way.' I wasn't patient enough for that, even though I recognise the wisdom of the advice. My pleasure in golf is whacking the ball. I find it therapeutic. If I hit only half a dozen shots in a round over 220 yards I'm still content – my best is a measured 310 yard drive (downhill in a dry season) at Roehampton. For me, scoring or even winning isn't the point. The joy is in a towering drive or fairway wood or seven-iron that comes right out of the meat of the club.

My father tells me that you lose five or ten yards a shot as you get older – he expects to be going backwards any day now. If so, the fun may begin to go out of it, but somehow I doubt that; I'll just have a better excuse for things going wrong.

Both my father and father-in-law play in octogenarian groups which their wives describe as 'Last of the Summer Wine'. These 'oldies' have their own grim brand of gallows humour, as I found when I overheard one of their favourite jokes: A golfing threesome was so regular that the barman knew exactly when to put out their whiskies. But one day they were late and only two of them entered the bar.

'What's happened?' asked the barman.

'It was Fred,' one of the players said. 'He died on the sixth tee.'

'You must have had a job carrying his body all the way back to the clubhouse.'

'It wasn't carrying him back that tired us,' said the man, sipping his whisky. 'It was all that picking him up and putting him down between shots on the way here.'

We had to wear red sweaters on Wimbledon Common to alert people walking their dogs. I used to find that my ball would find the walkers unerringly whenever I caught the faintest sight of them, even though I was aiming elsewhere. So much so that a partner once suggested that I should try keeping an old lady with a dog on every green or in the middle of the fairway.

I once played Len Hutton, the great cricketer, at Royal Wimbledon. He was then in his sixties. It was quite an education in golf

to see him hitting the ball, because his left arm was three inches shorter than the right after a war-time accident. As in his batting, he adjusted his style to compensate, using a three-quarter swing and concentrating on his short play. As I peppered the ball over London SW19 I would hear this gentle Yorkshire voice of admonition in my ear: 'It's all in the hands, Donald.'

He told me about cricketers and golf. There were those with a brilliant eye and strong shoulders, like Ted Dexter and Ian Botham, who were powerful off the tee. But his favourites were the artistic stroke-players such as Tom Graveney and Colin Cowdrey, who were immaculate in their iron play. From the experience of his own disability, he had come to disagree with pundits like Henry Longhurst who insisted that the secret of the successful golf swing lay in the legs. 'It's all in the hands, Donald.' I later found a comment by Bobby Jones that supported him: 'A golfer is only as good as his hands.'

I remember playing once in Morocco, where the King was said to be a keen player and used gallons of water on his private golf course when the people in the neighbouring village had no supply at all. He wasn't all that good at golf either, according to the pro who gave him lessons. There was one short hole on his course where the green was an island, crossed by a narrow bridge. I lost several balls in the water before I hit the target. The story goes that Billy Casper got so frustrated at missing the island green that he went down to the water's edge, took a three-iron and bounced his ball across on top of the lake.

When I arrived in Rabat, I found that all the hotels, including golf complexes, had been commandeered for an Arab Summit. When I had failed several times to get past a man on the gate, I finally spluttered: 'Who do you think you are?' He moved his jacket aside to reveal the pistol in his holster and said with an air of quiet menace: '*Je suis quelqu'un d'importance.*'

I still get a glow of self-importance myself when I look at a poster on my study wall. It's from the La Manga pro-am of 1973, and there I am on the same sheet as Tony Jacklin and Gary Player. Even the list of amateurs isn't too bad: Joe Di Maggio and Fred MacMurray, for example, and the former Wimbledon tennis champion, Manuel Santana, who was no slouch with the fairway woods, as I recall.

I played in a threesome with Dale Hayes, the South African pro, in a match where the amateurs' performance affected the amount of money the pro would get at the end of the day. This added an extra dimension of strain to what was already a nervy enough occasion. I remember missing one shortish putt and seeing the pro pick up my ball in his putter and hurl it thirty yards away into a lake. He didn't utter a single word. But I got the point.

My favourite golf hole is the seventh at Vale de Lobo in the Algarve. You tee off across a canyon which goes straight down to the Atlantic. If you fall short of the green, about 200 yards away, you're on rocky ground where the ball is quite unplayable. Behind the green it is much the same. So it's the green or nothing – or, more likely, the green or ten.

Mind you, I don't know that these acclaimed golfing architects, such as Robert Trent Jones, are really all they're cracked up to be. They have a nasty habit of putting artificial lakes just where my ball is about to land. When I lost all those balls at Marbella, I sent a postcard to a colleague at home with a message saying: 'Lost 14 balls. Is this par for the course?' He wrote back, having looked at the picture of the beach: 'I'm not surprised if this is what the bunkers are like.'

I heard of a golf course consultant who was summoned all the way to Japan at vast expense to solve a landscaping problem at a rich businessmen's club. The problem, they explained, was that members couldn't see the flag as they approached the green because of the lie of the land. What did he propose? He took one look and offered a solution they gladly adopted: make a longer flagpole.

I realise now that I should have played more in Africa when I was out there as a correspondent in the 1960s. I had friends who played golf in Kenya, Malawi and what was then Rhodesia. They were the final days of colonial splendour, with two caddies – one to carry your clubs and the other to mark your ball (and, if you were lucky, to nudge your ball out of the rough or fetch it out of the trees before you caught up).

But cheating of that sort would deprive us of one of the main benefits of playing golf badly – or so P. G. Wodehouse would have us believe. 'It is one of the chief merits of golf, that non-success at the game induces a certain amount of decent humility, which keeps a man from pluming himself on any petty triumphs he may achieve in other walks of life . . . Sudden success at golf is like the sudden acquisition of wealth. It is apt to unsettle and deteriorate the character . . .'

'Golf,' says the Oldest Member, ruminating on the terrace, 'acts as a corrective against sinful pride. I attribute the insane arrogance of the later Roman emperors almost entirely to the fact that, never having played golf, they never knew that strange chastening humility which is engendered by a topped chip shot. If Cleopatra had been ousted in the first round of the Ladies' Singles, we should have heard a lot less of her proud imperiousness.'

For myself, however, I seek no spurious moral justification for playing a game I enjoy – a game that also provides healthy exercise in attractive places. I subscribe to the enjoyment principle defined by my long-time golf correspondent Peter Dobereiner: 'Golf should not be a battle in the lifemanship war, or a virility test, or a social asset or an excuse for gambling, or a character-building hobby, or a reason for not taking the family out on Sundays, although it may contain elements of all of them. Essentially it is for amusement only. If it is played in that spirit it can be the most rewarding and satisfying game of them all and its fascination will endure for a lifetime.'

NOT BEFORE 8.30 P.M.

Sir Michael Davies

When I was a young barrister it was perfectly easy to make enough money out of undies each year to pay for the bringing up of at least one child. I'm not talking about undergarments, you understand, but undefended divorces. In those days, if a husband and wife wanted a divorce, they couldn't get it as they can today at a sort of judicial mail order warehouse. Indeed, any sort of agreement to divorce (if found out) was a disqualification and the parties stayed married. There had to be a hearing – a trial – in open court before a High Court judge or a lesser functionary acting as such for the day and rather pleased to be addressed as 'My Lord' instead of 'Your Honour'.

The petitioner – the spouse taking the active role – had to be represented by a barrister. A few simple questions craftily suggesting the answers without too obviously doing so, perhaps a short witness and then: 'On that evidence, My Lord, I ask for a decree nisi with costs against the respondent.' The decent judge – and most of them were – would respond 'Yes, Mr Davies,' and that was that. Anything between five and ten pounds for a few minutes' work into Mr Davies' pocket – and we're talking about the fifties, mind. With any luck, the judge would say 'Yes, Mr Davies, about fifteen times. A day like that once a month and the young barrister was on his way to comfortable solvency.

I know what you're thinking: what's this to do with golf? It isn't yet; but be patient.

There *was* sometimes a slight obstacle. Whatever the grounds for the petition – usually desertion, cruelty or adultery – if the petitioner had committed adultery he or she had to set out all the

details in a written statement. This was put into a sealed envelope
and towards the end of the petitioner's evidence his or her barrister
would solemnly announce: 'I put in the discretion statement'. The
Clerk of the Court with equal solemnity would open the envelope
and the paper was handed to the petitioner. The barrister would
then ask: 'Is that your signature? Do you remember signing that
statement? Is it true? Does it fully set out all acts of adultery
committed by you during the marriage?' If the petitioner failed to
answer 'Yes' to all four questions (and it happened sometimes)
then he or she didn't deserve a divorce anyway. If all went well,
then the barrister would insert into his plea the right words: 'I ask
in the exercise of the Court's discretion for a decree etc. etc.'
Discretion statements were ordinarily quite simple. The petitioner
in the traditional phrase was probably 'living, co-habiting and
frequently committing adultery with' one of the opposite sex, with
whom marriage was the ultimate aim.

This brings me to a petitioner client of mine who was really
responsible for my appearance later as counsel before the committee of the Redwoods Golf and Country Club with a well-paid
brief inscribed on the outside with the unusual words 'Not before
8.30 p.m.' Unusual, because courts and tribunals familiar to
lawyers are not expected to be in session at that hour. For twenty
years or more this petitioner client had been the professional at
the Redwoods Golf Club (let's drop the 'and Country'). He was
the old type of golf pro – tall, very substantially built, curly
gingerish hair, cricket ball complexion. Tweedy clothes. You don't
often see his type nowadays – these modern pros are all so young
and *dapper*, aren't they? He looked as though he should have been
called Sandy McMurdo. In fact, his name was Ambrose Smith.

Ambrose Smith had been a bit naughty. Over the years he had
committed adultery with no fewer than eighteen women – the
highest score ever achieved, or at least admitted to, by any client
of mine. What is more, each and every one of these willing ladies
was, and as far as I know remained, a member of the Redwoods
Golf Club. Like many pros in those and earlier days, Ambrose
lived with his wife literally over the shop and so his indiscretions
had taken place, no doubt, in the course of friendly teaching

rounds, at various private and convenient places on the links. I
say links, but happily for Ambrose's libido Redwoods is not a
treeless seaside course but is as its name suggests extensively
wooded. I believe Mrs Smith had never found out what her husband was up to from time to time – a few years earlier she had
pushed off and gone to live with her mother in Preston which,
although not the obligatory method, was as good a way of committing the 'matrimonial offence of desertion' as any other.

So there was Ambrose, with this bulky document – it looked
more the size of a golfing magazine than a discretion statement –
in his massive hands, giving a calm assent to all those questions
which I have told you were asked on these occasions. I wish I
could reveal that he added something wonderfully memorable like:
'My Lord, I only did it because it seemed to be good for my
putting' or 'My contract with the club obliged me to provide any
reasonable act of service required of me by any member', but he
didn't. Just 'Yes; yes; yes; yes'. I thought it better not to invite him
to elaborate. I fired the usual plea at the judge. He paused. There
were some signs of thought – maybe emotion – on his face. I
guessed he was thinking – ought I to make a fuss about this? Isn't
it making a mockery of the law that this wholesale adulterer should
be the one to be granted a decree? Then his face cleared. He
thought: What the hell! That Davies will be arguing with me for
half an hour and it won't do the wife or anyone else any good to
keep them tied together. So he said 'Yes, Mr Davies,' and the next
case was called on. He was a decent judge (handicap 9, I believe).

Ambrose Smith's solicitor was one Geoffrey Freebay. He prac-
tised in a modest way in a small town not far from the Redwoods
Golf Club. I think he made his living out of conveyancing and
wills – took on litigation only for people he already knew or were
personally recommended to him. Never got on his feet in Court,
never, which meant that he sent all his work to counsel: just the
kind of solicitor that young barristers like to see breeding freely.

Well, two or three years after Ambrose Smith's divorce, when
I'm glad to say my practice was progressing nicely, Mr Freebay
telephoned my Clerk to fix up a conference with me. He wanted
to bring his client, Mrs Amanda Mayfield, with him. My clerk

asked if there would be any written instructions for me in advance. 'No,' said Mr Freebay. 'Mrs Mayfield wants to explain everything to Mr Davies herself.' This is something barristers don't much like. It's much more satisfactory to know as much as possible in advance – otherwise, you start off at a bit of a disadvantage.

The day of the con came. My chambers were not in one of the Inns of Court in London where the leafy greenness makes one seem to be on the edge of a golf course, but in the middle of a large city in the industrial Midlands – 'where the iron heart of England beats, beneath her sombre robe', as the opening words of my old school song so felicitously put it. You could say that there's been some fibrillation in the iron heart in recent years, but that's by the way.

The only fibrillation on that May afternoon in the early 1960s was caused by Mrs Amanda Mayfield. An elderly barrister in my Chambers, who could have been the model for Uncle Tom in Rumpole, if you remember Uncle Tom, said to me later: 'Who was that? She's a real Humphry Clinker!'

And so she was. I'm no good at describing women – to me they're usually like goddesses or the back end of a diesel multiple unit. She was most certainly in the first category. You must have seen Catherine Deneuve, the French film actress. Well, Mrs Amanda Mayfield was exactly like Catherine Deneuve at her very best – except that she spoke in English, thank God. She must have looked much the same from her early twenties to her middle forties, which was her age group when she came to see me. Her summer dress was tightish, but not so tight as to be vulgar: short, but not so short as to be crude. All in all, a real stunner. Mr Freebay in his black coat (faintly powdered with dandruff) and striped trousers (yes, solicitors did wear that gear then – now they often favour unisex jeans) looked dim and I wished my collar was cleaner and that I wasn't already beginning to lose my hair.

Mr Freebay made the introductions. Mrs Mayfield was a member of the Redwoods Golf Club and 'had a problem upon which she desired the advice of counsel'. 'Amby Smith told me that you got him a divorce,' said Mrs Mayfield. 'He was very pleased with you.' Barristers have no memory of most of the cases they do the day after they're over, undies most of all, but not surprisingly I had not entirely forgotten Mr Smith's divorce. My mind raced back. Was she one of his eighteen conquests? Mrs Mayfield – my God, she was sharp as well as stunning – guessed what I was thinking almost before I had thought it. 'No,' she went on. 'I wasn't one of the eighteen holes he filled – he'd finished that round before I joined the club. And he's much too beefy anyway,' she added, gazing with apparent innocence at me. I felt rather pleased that I was over six feet but at the time weighed no more than ten stone. I could see that Mr Freebay thought it was time to get down to business – no doubt back at his office house buyers and will makers were queueing up for his attentions. 'It's like this,' he explained. 'Mrs Mayfield came to live at Redwoods a couple of years ago and joined the golf club.' I forgot to mention that he had already conveyed with delicacy – what diplomats experienced solicitors can be – that there was no longer a Mr Mayfield on the scene: whether dead or divorced I never knew, but he had left her 'in reasonably comfortable circumstances'. In solicitor-speak that meant that she was probably as well off as he and I put together and was certainly good for the fees.

Mr Freebay paused. He didn't seem to know quite where to begin the story. A lesser woman than Mrs Amanda Mayfield would have come to his rescue without being invited to do so, showing a kind heart but seeming to be assertive. Not she. Mrs Mayfield looked demurely down at the worn carpet in front of her. 'Er – well,' said Mr Freebay, 'Mrs Mayfield did want to explain the situation herself to you, sir' – I liked that 'sir': he must have been twenty years older than me – 'so perhaps . . .'

I looked at her: 'Mrs Mayfield?' She began – slowly and in what I've heard described as liquid tones. You know, they make the hearer's legs turn to water. 'I don't know what's the matter with them, Michael, the ladies at Redwoods all seem to hate me.'

'Why?'

'I don't know.' Of course she did.

Mr Freebay obviously thought that he'd better get her to the facts: 'Tell Mr Davies about the foursome you had with the Lady President and the Lady Captain and Colonel Mainwaring's wife.'

'Oh, yes – it was last year. I played with these three dreadful old girls – not one of them could have hit a cow's arse with a banjo – and when we got in they were dithering about in the changing room so I just went into the bar, and there was Jimmy Braithwaite, such a sweet man. He said, you know, just to make conversation, "Had a nice game?" I said, "No, I've just played with three old bags and we only had one womb between us – and that was mine." Now, tell me what was wrong with saying that. It was perfectly true.' She took out an expensive-looking cigarette case like ladies had in those 1930s black and white British movies you see on the television. She helped herself and handed me a gold lighter. A lesser woman (I know I've used those words before but they're so true) would have held my wrist and guided my hand to her cigarette. Not Mrs Amanda Mayfield. She let me light her cigarette. 'Smoke it for me, would you, darling, or put it out.' I did smoke in those days – but I put it out. I felt that the conference was getting rather out of my control. She returned to her tale and repeated: 'Well, what on earth was wrong with my saying that? But of course the bloody barman heard me. They call him the News of the World. He told the Captain of the club. He told the Lady Captain and there was the most God Almighty row.'

I waffled: 'But surely – an isolated incident – treat as a joke – laugh it off – apologise – forgive and forget – that sort of thing.'

'Well, that's what I would have thought,' responded Mrs Mayfield, 'but then there was the business with the Labrador.' She fixed me with her eyes, which managed somehow to be cool and burning at the same time.

'The Labrador?'

'Yes, it just happened to be the bloody Lady Captain again. Do you know our course? No? Well, like it often is, if you're sitting on the terrace outside the clubhouse you look down on the eighteenth green – you can see people putting out on it. They can see you – and hear you, as I found out,' she added mischievously.

'What happened?'

'This old trout, the Lady Captain, I mean, was just finishing a single. Can't remember who she was playing. Her Labrador was following her. She was about twenty yards short of the green. Just a little chip – down in two – easy. And do you know what that stupid woman did – you won't believe it.'

As a long handicap golfer – never been less than 18 in my life – I could guess.

'She fluffed it. The Lady Captain. Hit the ball about two feet.'

'And?'

'I was just sitting there on the terrace, having a couple of drinks with Jimmy Braithwaite, when we saw what I've just told you.'

I was beginning to know Mrs Amanda Mayfield: 'And you said something?'

'Yes, of course I did – who wouldn't? – although, honestly, I didn't mean her to hear it.' I believed her although, as they say, thousands wouldn't. 'I just said "Look, Jimmy, that was such a bloody awful chip that even her Labrador turned his back on it." And he had,' she finished cheerfully, as though that excused everything.

Tea came and went. Mr Freebay looked a little distrait but I was riveted as Mrs Amanda Mayfield went on and on. There were at least half a dozen more such stories. Always she seemed to have said something calculated to make the hearer – invariably a woman – furious. Like when she said in the hearing of the Lady President, who happened to be 72 years of age, 'The trouble with the women in this club is that they're all too old. Why, last year, when they had the Under 70s against the Over 70s match, the Under 70s couldn't even raise a team.'

At about six o'clock that evening – we'd started the con at half past four – I thought we really ought to get to the heart of the matter. 'So what *is* the problem?' I asked. The answer came at once. No hacking about in the bush for Mrs Amanda Mayfield. 'Michael, they've sacked me – expelled – membership terminated – pompous twits! I'm going to sue them – screw them for damages – get them all over the front page of the *Daily Mail*.' (We didn't have the modern *Sun* in those days.)

Now, this was interesting. When you get involved with the Common Law, you soon find out that without legal advice (and they seldom seek it) no organisation like a golf club, a trade union, a women's institute or whatever – or an employer for that matter

– can ever get rid of someone without making a real mess of it. Think of how many 'wrongful dismissal' cases you read about in the papers.

What had been the final straw was this. There'd been a Mixed Foursomes competition arranged one Sunday afternoon. Mrs Amanda Mayfield had been down to play with her friend Jimmy Braithwaite at 2.30 p.m. She hadn't turned up – no message, nothing. Neither had Jimmy. The other couple had been left with no opponents and had complained. When tackled about it, Mrs Amanda Mayfield had airily replied, 'But it was pissing down. Even in this bloody stupid club I wouldn't have thought anyone would have played in *that* rain.' If Mrs Amanda Mayfield had been a lesser woman (sorry!) I would have guessed that she was in bed at the time with Jimmy Braithwaite; but I'm sure she wasn't: that wouldn't have been stylish.

The Lady Captain had seen her chance. A quick meeting of the Ladies' Committee. That was about the only formality they got right. No notice of the meeting was given to the 'accused'. No notice of the 'charge'. No opportunity to put forward a defence. What about 'Natural Justice' then?

Mrs Amanda Mayfield had been all for issuing a writ at once and getting her case into court in three days – more like three years, I thought. But Mr Freebay had been cautious, as he now explained to me, leaning forward and quite enjoying the centre of the stage: 'Fortunately, Mr Davies, one of my brother solicitors – not very bright but quite straight – is on the main committee – the men's committee – of the club. A full hearing of the charge of "wilfully and without good reason not presenting herself on the first tee etc etc" has been arranged and Mrs Amanda Mayfield will be permitted to be represented by counsel. It will take place this day fortnight in the clubhouse at the Redwoods Golf Club, not before 8.30 p.m. Your clerk has been good enough to inform me that you are free that evening' (how the hell does he know that I'm free that *evening*? I thought), 'and we very much hope that you will accept the brief.'

'Please,' murmured Mrs Amanda Mayfield, and she made the word last for what seemed like 30 seconds.

And so it came about that two weeks later I drove up the tree-lined drive leading to the Redwoods Golf Club – I *know* it's a hackneyed phrase but the blessed thing *was* tree-lined – and met Mr Freebay and Mrs Amanda Mayfield in the hall. He had discarded his very formal wear for something faintly charcoal. Mrs Amanda Mayfield was wearing a little black number which had 'unostentatious wealth' written all over it. I had my brief marked 'Before the Committee of the Redwoods Golf Club. In the matter of Mrs Amanda Mayfield's wrongful expulsion. Not before 8.30 p.m. Mr Michael Davies of Counsel.' And then a satisfying figure – in guineas in those days of course.

Because this is a short story and a true story, you will have guessed that there is to be no Court Room Drama. After we had waited for a quarter of an hour, a messenger came out of the committee room: 'Would Mr Davies come in to see the committee – alone?'

'Yes, but only if my client agrees.'

'All right.' She did.

When I went in, there they were – ten men. The Captain in the chair. I recognised the Lady Captain's husband and Colonel Mainwaring from Mrs Amanda Mayfield's lively descriptions. The not very bright but straight solicitor – he *was* wearing his black coat and striped trousers – at the end, with a pile of papers in front of him. He never said a word. I was pleased to see that they all looked very uncomfortable.

The Captain spoke: 'Mr Davies, we have had the opportunity of discussing this unfortunate matter –'

Myself: 'You mean the wrongful expulsion of Mrs Amanda Mayfield?'

The Captain: 'Well, we needn't go into that at the moment. The long and short of it is that if your client is agreeable I am authorised on behalf of the club to tear up all the paper work in her presence' – he didn't seem to be able to bring himself to speak her name – 'and that of yourself and – er, um – Mr Freebay and to say that the termination of her membership is rescinded and she is reinstated as a member forthwith.'

After a pause, the Captain added, with an expression on his face which would have been fitting if he'd just missed a two-foot putt: 'And the club will undertake to pay all your client's legal costs to date, on condition that she agrees to take no further action in this matter.'

This was good enough for Mr Freebay and me. We didn't need to point out to Mrs Amanda Mayfield that publicity was rather vulgar. 'Of course, darlings, let's go in and enjoy watching them squirm. What a pity the Lady Captain isn't there. But old Rufus' – that was the Lady Captain's husband's name – 'he'll give her a blow-by-blow account.'

So in we went. Mrs Amanda Mayfield sat there looking more like Catherine Deneuve than ever. Colonel Mainwaring couldn't take his eyes off her. The Captain was as good as his word. He tore up the correspondence and put the papers into an enormous ash tray. He was fumbling for a match when Mrs Amanda Mayfield glided forward. 'My privilege, I think, gentlemen', she murmured, and lit a little bonfire with her gold lighter.

Afterwards she kissed me and said: 'I'm going now. Thank you – and would you give this to the Captain, please.' She handed me an envelope. 'It's my resignation from this bloody club. I've already joined' – and she mentioned another club not far away with a bit of a reputation for high living – 'and I've told this lot in my letter what I think of them. Ciao.'

I never saw her again. But what a woman – to me she will always be My Favourite Client.

Mr Freebay and I were invited into the men's bar. We had a drink – or two, no breathalyser then – and arranged to play golf with the Captain and Colonel Mainwaring at Redwoods the following Saturday.

LOVE–HATE

Edward Pearce

My relationship with golf is remote and vicarious. I don't play the game, though I would have quite liked to. All sports stand in defiance of my own nature, which has the co-ordination and balance of a bag of gravel. But I should have liked golf, might like it yet, at any rate the English sort. English golf, broadly speaking, takes place in scenery. It has been knocked about, driven through and improved somewhat by the landscapists. But compared to American golf, whose courses are triumphs of orthodonture, an English links is organic. The Americans favour Target Golf, a series of tee, trees, bunkers and hole, composed as one might paint by numbers, the whole of it given a final surface of laminate. Nothing eccentric obtains, nothing occurs by random chance. The presence of people on such a fictive landscape looks wrong, hence the preferred solution of filling them largely with Americans. They, resembling single sperm clonings, appear, like their golf courses, to belong on the same, distant planet.

Not that all of our golfing eccentricity is so endearing. The naming of individual holes by twee Scottish names has upthrowing potential. Bide a Wee, the Tappitt Hen, Wee Hamish's Ane Yin, Aa Didna Ken, The Immortal Memory, Daftie's Gang and the Sleekit Gerbil and other surreal craftings of unspeakable Harry Lauderish kitsch suggests the very opposite to the Scottish national instinct to take your legs off at the ankles. They amount to a gruesome pitch at the sympathy of overcharged tourists, a request that they tickle Scotland's belly with a putter.

Golf also has its social and political overtones. All sport is more or less right-wing, in that muscle tone and acceptance of authority go together: and within 'right-wing' one may include such places as the former German Democratic Republic and gruesome North Korea, places which turned or turn out high production numbers of skaters, runners and people who throw things. Pluralism doesn't go with games. The very expression 'team spirit' rings with conformity, shared striving, authority, and all the nightmare impulses of patriotism. Games are war-substitutes and there's an end of it.

Golf, however, like tennis, though not troubled over much by the team, also has a large element of the entrepreneurial. Businessmen play golf, and golf is played as a business. Amiable eccentrics like the left-wing trade unionist Hugh Scanlon, who has a passion for the links, are tolerated. But the emblematic man of golf is Mark McCormack, whose essence hovers among gatherings of professionals like the Holy Ghost among communicants. Golf is the game where men are weighed by earnings, the home of spin-offs, Faldo tee shirts, man-merchandising, the bloodless rustle of value-bearing pieces of paper. All of which is very nice, and better as a way of responding to talent than the old dependency of professional performer and gentleman patron. Better to be paid real money by McCormack than tipped by the Prince of Wales.

The game in those days, those of the last Prince of Wales (who actually was quite appalling himself), can have been no joy. They afforded the prince and his cronies the chance of being seen and admired ineffably wearing, and being proud of, a sort of deutero-trouser known as plus-twos or another called plus-fours (bagged and gathered in, either at the knee or halfway down the calf, the sort of costume which might be worn by Papageno in a Scottish setting of *The Magic Flute*). There was a strong case for finding golf intolerable for the simple reason that the last Prince of Wales gave up the melancholy and exiguous best of his mind and spirit to playing it. Perhaps the sleek commercial ripple of bought-and-sold, all-rights-marketed golf is a liberation.

But there is something very hard to take about the relentless ubiquity of it all, the way commentator, player and spectator seem to be bit players in a vast toy theatre given to McCormack by God, supposing that McCormack is not God. The commercial sport has an oceanic quality, the smarm of the in-house commentators lauding the in-house gladiators depresses. Though nothing depresses as that godless attempt to diversify the market 'pro-celebrity golf'. A witless comedian of the kind better stoned to death, Jimmy Tarbuck say, walks the links with a verbally con-stricted athlete without a script. And some heartlessly well-meaning footman walks with them watchful of the brutish eruptions of an unminded comic, attentive and supplemental to the deep silences of the sporting heavy. Over it all ticks the meter of money earned.

Enough mentally under-privileged owners of television sets tes-tify to the commercial viability of this combination of quarter-golf and non-conversation. There is no edge, no contest, no possible interest in the outcome of tee shot, sand escape or chip shot. It is not theatre, nor sport and bears the same relationship to entertain-ment as the resurrectable, to be heated-up thing in foil, to a cooked meal. Pro-celebrity golf is a small certain proof, like a cairn on a mountainside, of a civilisation in secular retreat.

Though the off-camera sort of encounter between dabbler and employee can have its grimly amusing moments, I, once and once only, walked round with a competition, the wretchedly ill-fated Bob Hope, run for the first and last time in Britain at Moor Park. This was the one where something very odd happened to the money and which will not be repeated. There was a variety, which is to say an identity, of stars and famous people involved, though one must except from all censure the great Henry Cooper, who is a very good amateur golfer. I had never seen him up close before and the reality was extraordinary, like seeing a wardrobe with matching pectorals. He was, and I bet still is, astonishingly and depressingly fit (evidence of the therapeutic effects of golf on top of road work), hit the ball straight and far and remained his old, placid, good-tempered and yet discreetly terrifying self. The thought occurs that the Terry character in *Minder* is a species of Henry Cooper with a line in wisecracks, a chivalric heavy in his own incorruptible class.

Rather different was Victor Matthews, not a bad chap actually, one for whom I worked happily enough years ago. Compared to his successors in the ownership of Express Newspapers, Victor

Matthews has most of the qualities of a Renaissance Prince, but
he isn't a very good golfer. I just happened to be there when Victor
hit a ball with firm address and a nice steady wrist, clean into the
upper branches of a tree, where it decided to stay, in contradistinc-
tion to Victor, who said something better not printed before
announcing that he was going home.

That of course could be anybody's game of golf, far away from
the tosh of a display match. Golf, like rain, descends upon the just
and the unjust alike, its puzzles unsolved, its ha-has fallen down,
its chip shots over-reached. There is room for dreadful Emersonian
musings on the affinities of golf with life. Emerson, remember,
was given to announcing that marriage was the tobacco in the
pipe of life. Faced with golf, which hadn't really taken off in the
Massachusetts of 1850 when Emerson was sorting things out, he
would have produced some hideous parallels all about adversity
being the drop shot of life or success rolling sweetly to within three
inches of the pin: he was like that.

But he would have had this much of a point. Golf, if no leveller,
is open to the talents. It is also a great finder out of fraud and
delusion. Back in his newspaper office Vic Matthews could have
called for exit from the European Community or abolition of the
Health Service (not that he would) and a servile editor, himself
obeyed by journalists servile to *him*, would have jumped to pro-
claim the doom of the false froggies with their evil bureaucracy
and the curse of pampering people with unwanted care. But on
the course if he drove his ball at a tree the tree would demo-
cratically stand its ground and spell out a rotten stroke as a rotten
stroke. If it had been an editor – and I have known several editors
who *were* trees – it would of course have hastened to put the
proprietor's ball two feet from the hole. As much would be true
if Mark McCormack drove at a tree, though we can be sure that
the attendant golfers, commentators and air fillers would do
loyally whatever the great man wanted, from laughing things off
to cutting it down.

For the rest of us, the immutability of wrong shots is a perma-
nent test of character, a modified form of the memento mori. And
indeed Golf is not like life as Emerson would have said if we had

given him the chance, so much as it is like death: death, that is, in Housman's sense of the Just City.

> The brisk fond lackey to fetch and carry,
> The true, sick-hearted slave
> Expect him not in the just city
> And free land of the grave.

No caddies after death; and indeed, no man four-putting can quite believe his own propaganda or disbelieve in his mortality. All of human fallibility is collected into the eighteen-inch putt trickling past or the chip going off the back of the green.

The obstacle quality of the game, the very Protestant requirement that the player solve his own problems, the priesthood of every scratch player, replicate the glitches and problems of life. And yet they are undertaken for pleasure. This says something interesting about human nature. There is an old, old *Punch* cartoon from a hundred years or more back. It involves dialogue between a shock-headed occupant of an asylum and a golfer. It went something like this:

Inmate: What are you doing?
Golfer: Trying to knock a ball through rough grass.
Inmate: And what will you do when it gets through?
Golfer: Try to knock it another hundred and fifty yards on to an earth platform with a hole in the middle.
Inmate: Who is making you do this?
Golfer: No one. I enjoy doing it.
Inmate: Come inside.

More than any other game golf invites humiliation among friends, socially disruptive competition, argument over a rule book of T and G dimensions, conclusive proof of one's lack of physical co-ordination, frustrated loss coupled with futile search, the company of knowing and mocking menials, traps which intimate boobydom and the raging dementia of successive near-misses. It is a game devised perhaps by psychologists consulting to business recruitment. The man able to endure the degradations of a middling round, to lose a ball with aplomb, mis-tee with equanimity, see trickle-past and re-trickle-past on the down slope off the green with simple grace is equipped for the highest places in British industry.

In fact, golfers themselves, the real competing ones, even though their skills obviate the worst happenings on the stations of the driver, do provide a running commentary on human character. The club smashers and throwers are deplored and discouraged, the perfect gentle knights exalted. Irony is at a premium. Men getting it right or wrong at a hundred thousand dollars a stroke to camera are developing character in ways not thought of by the Holy Inquisition. Arnold Palmer was a hero to a couple of generations, not only for excellent golf but for an Ohio phlegm (it was Ohio wasn't it?) which did to triumph and disaster all the things which Kipling so sententiously recommended.

Doug Sanders missing that putt in the British Open wasn't just giving us tragedy, he was like a character in a bad British film going to a German firing squad with a smile on his lips, a touch, if you like, of the Sydney Cartons. Personally I wouldn't mind seeing a golfer beating his caddy about the shoulders with a number five iron, but it smacks of verismo. There is probably a clause in the standard Mark McCormack contract voiding the agreement in such circumstances. The days of Norman von Nyder who used to break clubs over his knee are gone.

With the performer goes the commentator. Golf once had an antiquarian figure stretching back to the twenties, someone to whom Bobby Jones was a boyhood friend. This was Henry Longhurst, now dead. His voice practically wore plus-fours. It was a fruity, affably chuntering, old bufferish voice. It drew upon reminiscence fathoms deep, it spoke of golf in the days of gutta percha when men were men and sand-wedges were niblicks. It was like hearing about music from someone who had known Brahms or politics from a young admirer of Campbell-Bannerman. The shift to Peter Alliss has been imperceptible. A former player himself, Alliss is the embodiment of the chap who doesn't mind losing and loves the finer points. Actually an impressively nice chap, at any rate in all external appearance, he is the older sort of younger man in whom a shift of generation is hardly noticed. Together

with Harry Carpenter, he provides a cool, reassuring presence. Carpenter, though an excellent commentator, always seems to be looking for, or alternatively working up, the odd moment of atrocity readily at hand in his other trade, boxing.

Accustomed to cut eyes, men rising at eight, hasty patch-ups and resurrections in the corner and a state of affairs in which a clinch is the nearest you get to the walk down the fairway, Carpenter always seems faintly oppressed by the serenity of things. The civility of golf, its want of blood and serious injury must jar as much as it soothes, though Henry Cooper, a golfing temperament long employed fighting, is probably happy to be back with nothing more calamitous than long grass threatening him.

Golfing commentary is of necessity like cricket in needing any amount of informed time-filler. The sweet wittering arts of Brian Johnson remembering how Ponsford played the leg cut are very much in order and interestingly the Americans are not good at this. They are not much good at commentary actually, sounding at once eager, sycophantic and disembodied. Alternately they Caesarise the on-form dominator of the greens and the hour, otherwise falling back on endless visual aids flashing statistical digests on to the screen. They cannot ad-lib, they are in perpetual anxious assent with one another, cloned conformists who can't even master a conversation.

The British taste for comfortable reminiscence may be mocked, but it is human, it depends on a decent personal background in the game and a touch of human facility. The Americans, who so elevate their public commentators that they have even made a film (quite a good one, *Broadcast News*) about the gladiators of communication, report the sport from the shampooed and set handsomeness of Augusta or any of the replicas without quirk or flair. One expects to see a credit after transmission: Casting by Voxagolf Inc.

Our people may be young-bufferish (Alliss) or fighting that ulcer gamely (Carpenter), but they are human and thus ironically stars; frankly the American commentators are extras. Indeed the Stepford committee seem to have got at them. America suffers far beyond sport for elevating science-side skills and time and motion judgments above ungoverned, private, anarchic qualities. The cut and sliced vacuum-packed voices-over from the States are perfectly designed to report target golf from barbered identi-courses.

If Emerson were listening he might draw conclusions about human life, most of which has been wrung out of the American game. It is a vast, false, confected event for a programmed public who require not so much bread and circuses as crispbread and golf, a devitalised undertaking set in circumstances where the only animated things are the statistics. I'd sooner watch Victor Matthews swearing at a tree.

MANNERS AND CUSTOMS

Dame Joan Hammond

What caused raised eyebrows, frigid looks and acid comments at the Royal Melbourne Golf Club when golf for girls was in its embryonic stage? Playing golf bare-legged was forbidden; playing in slacks was absolutely barred; but it was neither of these that caused the upset.

My great friend and one-time golfing rival, Miss Odette Lefebvre, and I were in the New South Wales Ladies' Golf Union team to play interstate matches and compete in the Australian Ladies' Golf Championship, to be held at the RMGC. We decided not to stay with the team at a guest house near the course but to pay the extra and stay at a hotel in Melbourne. It was worth it, we felt, for the extra freedom.

We had been given directions to the course, by train and then by taxi at the other end. It seemed straightforward enough. We knew our starting times: we were first and second to be hitting off on the opening day, which meant an early start from Melbourne.

It was a very cold and frosty morning as we caught the first train to Sandringham. Well, we were early risers, so that was no problem, and the journey itself soon passed as we sat chatting of this and that and nothing in particular. We handed in our tickets at Sandringham, and casually asked the collector where we might find the taxi-rank.

'You'll be lucky if you find him about at this time of day,' he said, grinning. 'There's no rank: it's just him that takes people places, and he won't be around for another half-hour, I'd say.' He looked at our heavy golf bags and suitcases. 'If you're thinking of getting to the golf club you'll have to walk,' he added with a chuckle.

'How far?' we asked, concerned. Time was beginning to be of the greatest importance.

'Oh, I'd say about half an hour – if you move briskly,' he said with a laugh. He added an expressive but wholly unnecessary shrug of his shoulders and wandered off, still chuckling to himself.

This infuriated us as we realised what a helpless situation we were in. There we were, rapidly becoming desperate at the predicament we were in, while he thought it was a nice joke to start the day off with.

We *had* to be on the first tee in time. We went out into the street. No sign of life.

No one to be seen, and time ticking relentlessly away. Misery! What disgrace we would bring down on our team. It was unbearable, unthinkable. Not to be able to get to the club when we were so near – and, to make it bitterer still, in good time, until this unforeseen calamity had struck us. We wished fervently that we had stayed at the guest house with the others: but it was far too late for recriminations or regrets.

All in all, two more dejected golfers would have been hard to find in the State of Victoria at that moment, and, indeed, we were on the point of tears when, suddenly, coming slowly round the corner about a hundred yards up the road from where we stood, came salvation.

We stood for a moment, unable to move and staring in wonder. Oh, joy! Oh, joy of joys! Here was *transport*. And then, as one, we gathered up our bags and ran for all we were worth towards . . . the Sandringham milk cart.

The milkman had already taken a crate of milk into a house when we spied it, while the horse meandered peacefully along, pausing to munch grass from the verge. At any other time I would have found it a pleasant scene to watch, pastoral and soothing.

Out came the milkman carrying an empty crate. We greeted him with a *very* cheery 'Good morning,' and he returned it with a smile, which was encouraging. I acted as spokesman. Odette was my senior, but she had a slight stammer, which became more pronounced when she was upset. I should perhaps have explained also that she was half-French and half-Belgian. Many of her friends called her Frenchie, as a term of endearment, because of her strong French accent. It was very attractive, but not easy to follow when she was in the grip of some strong emotion.

I explained our unfortunate position and asked the milkman if he could possibly take us out to the golf course. 'Much as I'd like to, Miss, I can't,' he said. 'I'd be behind with my deliveries. I've never been behind,' he added simply, swinging the empty crate on to the cart.

I offered him money. He waved it derisively – almost contemptuously – aside. We were getting desperate. I told him we were visitors from New South Wales, and *that* didn't impress him a whole lot. Then I had an inspiration. I told him that we would disgrace our team if we failed to get on the first tee on time. We would be heartbroken, because we were the two top players.

At that moment we were both close to tears. I don't know which of the two things – the arguments or the incipient tears – worked the oracle; but one of them did. At least, something did. 'You're champs, playing in the Championship?' he said. 'Why didn't you tell me before? C'mon, git aboard. Me'n Blackie'll git you there.'

He lodged our clubs and bags among the crates and the three of us climbed aboard. It was a squash, and the narrow wooden seat was very hard, but we were, at least, in motion. We jogged and jolted along, accompanied by many a rousing shout to Blackie to 'Git along now!' Blackie was by no means used to the notion of a straight-out trot from here to there: milkmen's horses are accustomed to getting from A to C way of Z, if not 9, rather than a straightforward and simplistic B. He showed his displeasure by switching his tail madly in front of our faces, which resulted in our not being able to look at each other for the entire journey. Odette being one of those people who are always on the look-out for a laugh – not to say a horse laugh – we were constantly in terror that Blackie might forget, during one of his prodigious swishes, that ladies were present.

After what seemed like an eternity, we slowly turned into the drive leading to the front door of the club house. It was then, and then only, oddly enough, that we thought about the effect our means of transport might have on anyone seeing our stately arrival.

Under the eyes of three utterly bewildered ALGU officials we alighted with what dignity we could. Odette, with true Gallic *chic*, descended as if she was stepping out of a Rolls-Royce, our milkman her chauffeur. He played his part to perfection, clearly much taken by his charming foreign passenger. And I, meanwhile, suddenly thought of a certain operatic scene, and started to laugh. Odette, conscious of the ever-increasing number of eyes watching us, asked what in the world I could find funny in such a state of affairs. And I just laughed harder.

We said goodbye to our milkman, thanking him warmly and shaking his hand. He for his part doffed his cap like a junior member of the chorus hoping to be noticed, and said, with evident sincerity, that it had been his pleasure to meet us and help us.

We then hurried into the club house with a brisk 'Good morning' that was hardly proof against the chilly disapprobation in the air. Whatever else there may have been, there was, on the faces of the Golf Union officials, nothing whatever of the milk of human kindness. What we got was a sort of grunt of reply, and a look of ill-concealed incredulity at such profligately unbecoming behaviour. Entering the locker room we heard a loud, high-pitched voice squeaking, 'My dear, they were even *thanking* him, and SHAKING HIS HAND. It's so *embarrassing* for the club.'

We were suddenly recognised, and the babble of voices ceased. We ignored them, changed our shoes, and made for the first tee. There was no time for a preliminary hit: we were only just in time to be called to the tee. As we went round we were both aware that our troubles were only beginning: we had committed what was known as a foozle: a social gaffe of near-calamitous proportions.

Our spirits rallied more than a little, however, after we both won our matches.

Most of the officials and players were having tea when our Captain and one of the NSW LGU officials took us aside and quietly asked us what had happened. When we told them, they were, at last, sympathetic and understanding of the predicament in which we had found ourselves. They could not, indeed, have been nicer, and I thought I detected, along with the sympathy, a certain hint of amusement as the tale unfolded. At all events, they reassured us that we need not worry unduly, and that they would explain the circumstances of our less than dignified arrival at the mighty portals of the club.

The happy outcome of it all was that someone was deputed to collect us from our hotel in the mornings thereafter, and to take us back there in the evenings, though whether this was to make life as easy as possible for us or to ensure no further unorthodox modes of arrival and consequent embarrassment for a socially-conscious MGC I have no way of telling.

I had no chance to speak to Odette for some time after that, but the next time we did meet she was consumed with curiosity to know what had made me start laughing at the worst possible moment as we arrived. After a certain amount of humming and hawing, during which I chaffed her for her virtually total ignorance of, and indifference to, all things operatic, I mentioned that I had just been reading through some libretti, including that of Puccini's *La Bohème*. 'The scene is set,' I said, 'at one of the city toll-gates of Paris: the Barrière d'Enfer.'

'I know that part of Paris well,' she said.

So I told her how the morning is freezing, and all the customs officers are sitting round a coal brazier, when the curtains rise and some women come on to stage. An officer looks up and calls out 'Here come the women with their milk.'

There was a moment's silence. Then she said 'Y . . . Y . . . You'd b . . . b . . . better not give up your day j . . . j . . . job, you know.' It was the first time she'd stammered all day.

Nor was this the only time I found myself flummoxed and floundering in a golfing context. There was less excuse the next time, because I was an old hand, and the cause was nothing more than an opponent using a little of the art of gamesmanship on me.

It was a perfect day for golf. A slight breeze was blowing, just enough to keep you cool, and the sun was dodging behind puffs of cloud enough to stop it from being an irritant to the eyes on certain holes: what could be called a typical English summer's day. It suited me, and in all I felt that this was going to be *my* day. For I had been chosen to play in a county match, and was feeling mightily honoured, as it was the first time. Club matches were one thing, but to represent your club in a county match was, for me, a great event. Another good thing was that I was free, with no singing engagement to keep me from my golf date.

I had never met my opponent before. This was not surprising, because I was rarely available, even for club matches. It was the purest luck whether my professional singing dates fitted in with golfing activities: rehearsals and performances couldn't be scheduled to suit playing times, much though I often wished they could – there were many times when I longed to be out playing golf; a false and altogether absurd desire. I lived for my work, and it absorbed me totally; but those odd games of golf provided a very necessary distraction for a few hours now and then, enabling me to study for long periods without tiring. Especially at times when I was learning songs or opera by heart and having to spend long hours rehearsing, I found that if I could slip away for a couple of hours and play a few holes of golf I would return to work reinvigorated, batteries recharged and feeling refreshed and ready for more work.

As I said, I had never met my opponent; but one of our team members warned me that she had a reputation of being a formidable match player, who hardly said a word, but that, when she did, it was likely to be some comment aimed at putting you off the stroke you were about to play.

I've often felt self-conscious when playing a golf match with a stranger, especially watching for their reactions when they found out that I was the singer. The attitude would usually change either to awe or to an over-familiar hail-fellow-well-met – 'Oh, I *am* looking forward to playing with you.'

Now I was, at that time, a very popular classical singer, and my recording of 'Oh, my Beloved Father' was Top of the Pops in the UK. As I chatted to my opponent for that day before we started out, however, she appeared entirely indifferent to my reputation

– though I was told later that actually, because of it she hadn't been looking forward to our game, which was a shame.

In any case, once the match began I quite forgot about that brief conversation. My concentration was such that I'd more or less forgotten her existence. I was happy. I was playing well, and as we approached the fifteenth hole I was four up. Dormy 4. Very cosy. The scent of victory was already strong in my nostrils. But, like many a player before me, I fell into the old trap, and forgot that most vital reminder: the game is never lost until it's won.

So I stepped on to the fifteenth tee.

'I believe you know Joan Sutherland?' remarked my opponent. 'Wasn't it fantastic, the way she took over the *Lucia* role?' she went on without waiting for a reply. 'Her name on everyone's lips. The two Joans,' she trilled. 'Instead of Joan Hammond we now have Joan Sutherland. You must tell me what she's really like. And how exciting for you to have a fellow-Australian reach the dizzy heights . . .'

I jammed the tee into the ground and banged my ball down on it, breathing hard and wondering what was coming next in Sutherland broadsides. She generously paused for breath and allowed me to hit it. I played my first bad shot of the day.

I lost the 15th. I lost the 16th and the 17th. She never let up, and I was reacting like a beginner, at the very moment when I needed nothing so much as to control myself sufficiently to regain concentration to halve one hole. Win or halve the last hole, that was the only thing that mattered. Lose it, and the match would be halved, and I would be sickened. The team wanted a win, not a half. It was just as well my thoughts weren't being broadcast. They weren't of the pleasantest.

As I recall, my thoughts strayed to Stephen Potter and *The Theory and Practice of Gamesmanship*. A friend had lent it to me with a strong recommendation to study it well, there being so many players anxious to try it out on a real, live opponent. 'Strange old world. Even a game can be defiled,' I mused, letting my mind drift and whacking one of my best approach shots to the 18th. I holed the putt and won my match. I started breathing again, and thinking up a few questions of my own.

We shook hands and exchanged the usual pleasantries. Then as we walked to the club-house I asked, as casually as I could, how it was that she had suddenly become so talkative on the subject of Joan Sutherland.

'Stupid me,' she said flatly. 'My husband told me at breakfast to bombard you with questions about Sutherland. He said I'd get the better of you, because you'd be expecting me to rave about *you*. I forgot about it until it was too late – but it certainly knocked your concentration about when I woke up,' she said cheerfully. 'He said I'd win if I used gamesmanship,' she rattled on. 'It's quite legal, he said, and it can be fun watching your opponent lose concentration and start playing like an idiot. Cuts them down to size,' he said.

'Your husband sounds like a very *versatile* golfer,' I said, speaking, I rather think, through clenched teeth.

'A half would have been so much better than a loss,' she said. 'He'll have something to say about it when I tell him. He said you'd be sure to lose your grip once Joan Sutherland's name was mentioned.' And that was the climax and end of *my* day. It just shows how little the weather has to do with your game.

It didn't end sourly, however. Some time later I gave an abbreviated account of this incident in an after-dinner speech at which Joan Sutherland was present. I finished it off by saying how greatly I admired her (we'd known each other for years), and, on the other hand, how, for that one occasion only, I could have wrung her innocent neck; whereupon Joan, being the delightful person she is, threw back her head and laughed.

Tips on a Trip

John Updike

This piece is taken from Picked Up Pieces (Knopf, 1976)

I have been asked to write about golf as a hobby. But of course golf is not a hobby. Hobbies take place in the cellar and smell of airplane glue. Nor is golf, though some men turn it into such, meant to be a profession or a pleasure. Indeed, few sights are more odious on the golf course than a sauntering, beered-up foursome obviously having a good time. Some golfers, we are told, enjoy the landscape; but properly the landscape shrivels and compresses into the grim, surrealistically vivid patch of grass directly under the golfer's eyes as he morosely walks toward where he thinks his ball might be. We should be conscious of no more grass, the old Scots adage goes, than will cover our own graves. If neither work nor play, if more pain than pleasure but not essentially either, what, then, can golf be? Luckily, a word newly coined rings on the blank Formica of the conundrum. Golf is a *trip*.

A non-chemical hallucinogen, golf breaks the human body into components so strangely elongated and so tenuously linked, yet with anxious little bunches of hyper-consciousness and undue effort bulging here and there, along with rotating blind patches and a sort of cartilaginous euphoria – golf so transforms one's somatic sense, in short, that truth itself seems about to break through the exacerbated and as it were debunked fabric of mundane reality.

An exceedingly small ball is placed a large distance from one's face, and a silver wand curiously warped at one end is placed in one's hands. Additionally, one's head is set a-flitting with a swarm of dimly remembered 'tips'. Tommy Armour says to hit the ball with the right hand. Ben Hogan says to push off with the right foot. Arnold Palmer says keep your head still. Arnold Palmer has painted hands in his golf book. Gary Player says *don't* lift the left heel. There is a white circle around his heel. Dick Aultman says keep everything square, even your right foot to the line of flight. His book is full of beautiful pictures of straight lines lying along wrists like carpenter's rules on planed wood. Mindy Blake, in *his* golf book, says 'square-to-square' is an evolutionary half-step on the way to a stance in which both feet are skewed toward the hole and at the extremity of the backswing the angle between the left arm and the line to the target is a mere 14 degrees. Not 15 degrees. Not 13 degrees. Fourteen degrees. Jack Nicklaus, who is a big man, says you should stand up to the ball the way you'd stand around doing nothing in particular. Hogan and Player, who are small men, show a lot of strenuous arrows generating terrific torque at the hips. Player says pass the right shoulder under the chin. Somebody else says count two knuckles on the left hand at address. Somebody else says *no* knuckle should show. Which is to say nothing about knees, open or closed clubface at top of back-swing, passive right side, 'sitting down' to the ball, looking at the ball with the right eye – all of which are crucial.

This unpleasant paragraph above, strange to say, got me so excited I had to rush out into the yard and hit a few shots, even though it was pitch dark, and only the daffodils showed. Golf converts oddly well into words. Wodehouse's golf stories delighted me years before I touched a club. The story of Jones's Grand Slam, and Vardon's triumph over J. H. Taylor at Muirfield in 1896, and Palmer's catching Mike Souchak at Cherry Hills in 1960, are always enthralling – as is, indeed, the anecdote of the most abject duffer. For example:

Once, my head buzzing with a mess of anatomical and aero-nautical information that was not relating to the golf balls I was hitting, I went to a pro and had a lesson. Put your weight on the right foot, the man told me, and then the left. 'That's all?' I asked. 'That's all,' he said. 'What about the wrists pronating?' I asked. 'What about the angle of shoulder-plane vis-à-vis that of hip-

plane?' 'Forget them,' he said. Ironically, then, in order to demonstrate to him the folly of his command (much as the Six Hundred
rode into the valley of Death), I obeyed. The ball clicked into the
air, soared straight as a string, and fell in a distant ecstasy of
backspin. For some weeks, harboring this absurd instruction, I
went around golf courses like a giant, pounding out pars, humiliating my friends. But I never could identify with my new prowess;
I couldn't *internalise* it. There was an immense semi-circular area,
transparent, mysterious, anesthetised, above the monotonous
weight-shift of my feet. All richness had fled the game. So gradually
I went back on my lessons, ignored my feet, made a number of
other studied adjustments, and restored my swing to its original,
fascinating *terribilità*.

Like that golf story of mine? Let me tell you another: the greatest
shot of my life. It was years ago, on a little dog-leg left, downhill.
Apple trees were in blossom. Or the maples were turning; I forget
which. My drive was badly smothered, and after some painful
wounded bounces found rest in the deep rough at the crook of the
dog-leg. My second shot, a 9-iron too tensely gripped, moved a
great deal of grass. The third shot, a smoother swing with the
knees nicely flexed, nudged the ball a good six feet out on to the
fairway. The lie was downhill. The distance to the green was
perhaps 230 yards at this point. I chose (of course) a 3-wood. The
lie was not only downhill but sidehill. I tried to remember some
tip about sidehill lies; it was either (1) play the ball farther forward
from the center of the stance, with the stance more open, or (2)
play the ball farther back, off a closed stance, or (3) some combination. I compromised by swinging with locked elbows and looking up quickly, to see how it turned out. A divot the size of an
undershirt was taken some 18 inches behind the ball. The ball
moved a few puzzled inches. *Now here comes my great shot.*
Perfectly demented by frustration, I swung as if the club were an
ax with which I was reducing an orange crate to kindling wood.
Emitting a sucking, oval sound, the astounded ball, smitten, soared
far up the fairway, curling toward the fat part of the green with
just the daintiest trace of a fade, hit once on the fringe, kicked
smartly toward the flagstick, and stopped two feet from the cup.

I sank the putt for what my partner justly termed a 'remarkable six'.

In this mystical experience, some deep golf revelation was doubtless offered me, but I have never been able to grasp it, or to duplicate the shot. In fact, the only two golf tips I have found consistently useful are these. One (from Jack Nicklaus): on long putts, think of yourself putting the ball half the distance and having it roll the rest of the way. Two (from I forget – Mac Divot?): on chip shots, to keep from underhitting, imagine yourself *throwing* the ball to the green with the right hand.

Otherwise, though once in a while a 7-iron rips off the clubface with that pleasant tearing sound, as if pulling a zipper in space, and falls toward the hole like a raindrop down a well; or a drive draws sweetly with the bend of the fairway and disappears, still rolling, far beyond the applauding sprinkler, these things happen in spite of me, and not because of me. On the golf course as nowhere else, the tyranny of causalty is suspended, and men are free.

JOIN THE CLUB

Brian Glanville

The following piece first appeared in The Thing He Loves (1973)

I took a few lessons first, I wanted to see if I could play, if I could hit a ball, and I could. The professional at the department store said I'd got a natural swing. They lay it on a bit thick, I know, but I could feel for myself, I'd still got the eye.

In fact I'd played most games at one time or another: football, tennis, cricket, even a bit of cross-country running, only now I was past all that. I needed something else, and I thought: golf. I mean, at least it kept you out in the open, and then it was sociable, as well. So I bought a bag of clubs, and of course the next thing you do, you want to join a golf club.

People said, 'Join Mill Lodge,' that was the Jewish club, out in Hertfordshire. I said, 'Why should I join Mill Lodge? There's half a dozen that are nearer.' They said, 'You'll have trouble.' I said, 'All right, I'll have trouble.' I'd heard all that, but I suppose I didn't take it seriously: I mean, what trouble did I ever have in football or cricket?

The first club I tried was Brook Park, that was the nearest. I had a friend there, Willy Rose. He said, 'I'll sponsor you.' So for six weeks I played there, that was the probation period. The secretary said, 'You'll see if you like us, and we'll see if we like you.' He was retired from the Civil Service. He said, 'Quite frankly, Mr Richards, I can usually tell by looking at a person. What profession are you in?'

I said, 'I'm in the furniture business.'

Willy told me, 'He's a *momser*. They all are.' Still, I enjoyed playing there. It was a nice course. I usually played in a foursome with Willy and a couple of friends of his; now and again I'd join up with some of the other members. They were all right, quite friendly, though I didn't go for all that boozing in the bar, afterwards. Willy said, 'Listen, they're like that, you won't change them. That's the way they live.'

But I was hitting the ball well, I was improving. If they let me play there, they could drink as much as they liked.

After six weeks, I went to see the secretary. I said, 'Well, I've decided I'd like to join.'

He said, 'I see.' There was something changed about him. He was one of those lean men with a very clipped way of speaking and a little moustache, the kind of person that never seems to open up. He said, 'You've been playing mostly with Mr Rose, haven't you?'

I said, 'That's right. Mr Rose was sponsoring me.'

He said, 'Mr Richards, are you a Jew?'

I said, 'Yes, I am, as a matter of fact, but what's that got to do with playing golf?'

'I'm afraid we have a Jewish quota,' he said.

I said, 'What does that mean?' He said, 'It means we can't admit you.' I said, 'I see.'

To tell the truth, I couldn't believe it was happening. I'd got this numb feeling, all dazed, as though I was dreaming it. I said, 'Well, can't you put me on the waiting list?' I could hear myself speak; it didn't sound like my voice.

He said, 'There really wouldn't be much point.'

'Why not?' I asked. He said, 'The list's interminable.'

I said, 'Well, there's nothing more to discuss, then, is there?' I stood up, I didn't shake hands with him, then when I got to the door he asked me, 'Mr Richards, is Mr Rose a Jew?'

I said, 'I'm sorry, Mr Peters, I'm afraid I've always made it a practice in my business life never to inquire into a man's race or religion.' He could start his own bloody pogroms.

But that was only the beginning of it. If I told you the humiliations I had to put up with, the indignities they rained on me in those eighteen months, you'd never believe me. To begin with,

I didn't believe it, myself. But it only made me more determined.

The next club I tried turned out worse than the first: Regent's
Hill. And it all started out so well. I went to see the secretary and
he was very nice, charming; not like the first fellow. He wore a
check tweed suit and laughed a lot. He said, 'Fine, come along
and play, play here for a month, you're sure to find a couple of
sponsors.'

So I played and I was still doing well. I hadn't got a handicap
yet, but my scores were coming down all the time. The people
were all right, quite pleasant, bank managers and local businessmen and things like that. We hadn't got a lot to talk about,
but who cared? I'd come to play golf, conversation I could get
at home.

Then the month was up, and I went to see the secretary again.
He was still the same, he'd always been very friendly. He said,
'Oh, hallo, Mr Richards, you'll want your entry form now, won't
you?'

'Yes, please,' I said.

He said, 'Here you are,' then, just as I was leaving, he stopped
me. He said, 'One question,' and I thought, 'Here it comes.' I got
that feeling in my stomach. 'What's that?' I asked. He said, 'When
you're a member will you ask me to play?'

I drove back to town. I thought, that's fine. Then, when I got
home, I had a look at the form, and there it was. Question eleven:
religion; just like a kick in the guts.

For days I did nothing. Ten days, and I couldn't make up my
mind. The form just lay there, and I never touched it. In the end,
I rang him up. I said, 'It's Lionel Richards.' He said, 'Yes! You
haven't sent your form back yet.'

I said, 'No, I haven't. As a matter of fact there's one question
that's bothering me. I don't know what to make of it.'

'Really?' he said. 'Which one's that?'

'Number eleven,' I said, 'religion.'

'Oh,' he said, 'we only put that in to keep the Jews out.'

I got that feeling again, like somebody hitting you below the
belt. 'Well,' I said, 'I'm very sorry, but I *am* a Jew,' and he started

talking very quickly. 'It's not my rule, I didn't make it, it's made by the committee.'

'I see,' I said. 'Well, thank you very much.'

I nearly gave up, then. My wife was begging me to. She said, 'It's making you ill. What do you want to bother for?'

And my partner said, 'Look, if you want to play golf, join Mill Lodge.' 'I don't want to join Mill Lodge,' I said. 'Why should I join Mill Lodge?' He said, 'What's *wrong* with Mill Lodge? All right, so it's a bit expensive.' I said, 'That's got nothing to do with it. I'm not going to be *forced* to join Mill Lodge. If I join it, I'll join it of my own free will.' A month later he said, 'Look, you're driving me crackers with this. Join Mill Lodge! I'll propose you; I'll pay the bloody subscription for you!' I said, 'No,' because now I was determined. I said, 'I won't be able to live with myself.'

Somebody said, 'Why don't you try Muswell Park?' I went there and took one look at the secretary and I knew. He was a Colonel something-or-other, half of them were; they looked at you as if you were up on a court martial. He took out the form, he said, 'Religion?' I told him, and that was that: 'We'll phone you.' Of course, I never heard another word.

All over North London I tried, everywhere except the municipal courses. There was one club that gave me a two-month trial. After three weeks the secretary called me in. He looked embarrassed, I'll give him that. He said, 'I hope you don't mind my asking, Mr Richards, but it's been suggested to me you might be Jewish.'

I said, 'Suggested? Who suggested it?'

'As a matter of fact,' he said, 'it was one of our members.'

'Well, he was quite right,' I said. 'And now I suppose you're going to tell me you've got a quota. Don't worry, I'll leave; I'll leave now.'

He said, 'Please don't regard it as anything personal.'

'What do you want me to think?' I asked him. 'If it's nothing personal, why won't you have me?'

'It's the rule,' he said. But I'd lost my temper, I'd had too much of it. 'Rules just don't suddenly appear,' I said. 'Someone has to make them. Are they afraid I'll throw my ball out of the rough? Are they afraid I'll kick it into the hole when no one's looking?'

'Mr Richards,' he said, 'I keep telling you, there's nothing personal in it at all. It's just that *some* Jews . . .'

I said, 'What Jews?'

'Not people like you,' he said.

I said, 'How can you know what they're like when you won't let them play here?'

Another of them, another secretary, said, 'You Jews have *your* golf clubs, Mr Richards, and we have *our* clubs.'

I said, 'Yes, and *why* do we have our clubs? Because you won't let us join *your* clubs.'

I can tell you, there were times when I felt like giving up, throwing my clubs away, joining Mill Lodge after all, anything. I'd stand at the bar in these golf clubs, I'd look around at the members drinking there, or I'd see them in the locker room, and I'd think, what's the matter with us? What have they got against us? What's so different about us? And I found myself beginning to dislike them. Before, I'd detested the secretaries, but after all, what were the secretaries doing, only what they were told by these others. I didn't enjoy playing any more. I could only think, if they knew, they wouldn't play with me, so I began anticipating it. I'd call on the secretaries and I'd say, 'Before we start, I want to tell you that I'm Jewish. It doesn't make any difference to me, it may make a difference to you.' Then they'd say, 'We'll get in touch with you,' or, if they were honest, 'I'm afraid there's a quota.'

But I was going to beat them, whatever it cost me, and in the end, I did it in a funny way. There was a fellow I did business with, a wholesaler. One day we were talking, and he was going to Scotland on a golfing holiday. He said, 'Do you play?'

I said, 'When they let me.'

He said, 'What do you mean?' and I told him the story; he wasn't Jewish. He said, 'I've never heard anything so ridiculous. Why don't you come to *my* club? I'll put you up.' He told me the name, and I said, 'I've tried it, don't worry, I've tried every club in North London.'

'Have you tried Three Elms?' he said. It was a bit farther out, in Middlesex. 'No,' I said. 'It'll be just the same, though.'

'No it won't,' he said. 'I've got a friend there. He's the captain; if *he* puts you up, you're as good as in, it doesn't matter who you are or what you are.'

So we had lunch together, the three of us. His friend was quite a nice fellow, he was in plastics. He said, 'Of course we'll have you. No problem. Come on down: we'll play a round with the secretary.'

Which I did: it was a very nice club. They'd got religion on the form but I filled it in, the captain proposed me, and in a couple of weeks I got a letter; I'd been accepted. I played there six months on and off, they were all quite pleasant to me; then I resigned.

The secretary said, 'What's the matter, Mr Richards, aren't you happy here?'

'Oh, yes,' I said, 'it's nothing personal; I'd just like to give someone else a chance on the quota.'

So then I joined Mill Lodge. I'd proved my point.

Early Retirement

Miles Kington

Along with tennis, darts and bridge, golf is one of those games which you can supposedly play well into old age without suffering ill effects or getting sick of it. It is also a safe game, unlike those in which the winner is the best at inflicting physical damage on his opponent, such as boxing, car racing and rugby. This means that golfers go on playing until their dying day. And that means that they seldom tell their life story. Writing down your life story is an admission that you have come to the end of your active life, and no golfer seems prepared to do that.

Well, I find myself in the peculiar position of having played golf until the age of twenty and then given up. It wasn't that I disliked the game. I enjoyed it very much. I even got quite good at it. No, the fact was that by the age of twenty I seemed to have spent most of my leisure time playing golf and it was time to do something else. I now realise, looking back, that I was one of the rare people who crowded all his golfing days into the first end of his life, not the second part of it, and that I am therefore in the equally rare position of being able to write a golf autobiography with the full benefit of hindsight.

The reason I got into golf early in life was that my father needed an opponent. My father was, unlike me, a far-sighted businessman who planned ahead, and he could foresee a time when the man against whom he usually played on Sunday, Uncle Sidney, would find something better to do, or die, or emigrate, or get religion. (In fact he moved to the Isle of Man for tax reasons, which I suppose is a mixture of emigrating and dying.) Therefore he made sure that I got golf lessons from an early age and became good enough to step into Uncle Sidney's brogues.

The man who had the hapless task of teaching golf to me was Mr John Powell, the professional at the local club, which was Wrexham in North Wales. I say 'hapless task' not because I was a bad pupil, but because it quickly became apparent that golf is an unteachable game. Looking back, I see now that golf is designed for some alien being who has not yet been found, and teaching it is rather like trying to wrap a stupidly shaped Christmas present in a piece of wrapping paper too small for it: as soon as you've got one piece covered, another pops out. 'We've got the wrists rolling over nicely now,' poor Mr Powell would say, 'but you're turning too fast again,' or, 'Nice follow through, but the back swing is getting too fast again.' I once read a piece by Chris Plumridge in which he claimed that people who had slight physical disabilities (one leg shorter than the other, for instance) were more suited to golf than normal people, and I am prepared to believe it.

My father finally removed me from golf lessons when he judged that I was good enough to play him but not good enough to beat him, and at about the age of twelve or thirteen I finally got down to the real challenge of grown-up golf: being able to carry a heavy bag of clubs round eighteen holes. Although not a mountainous course, Wrexham was not one of your flat, easy English courses either and there seemed to be a great deal of up and down walking through some very pleasant landscape. That was another thing about golf I learnt early on: that very little of the game is spent actually tackling a ball and trying to put it somewhere else: you spend 99 per cent of the time walking, so it might as well be a nice walk.

It was on this principle that my father also organised our holidays, and for a long time we would only go away to places that had a nice golf course, or a famous one, or even a nice, famous one. In 1947, when I was six years old, we went on holiday to Northern Ireland, a place not favoured by many people for a summer break, even then, and it wasn't until years later that I realised it was the lure of Newcastle golf course by the sea, under the Mountains of Mourne, that had taken us there. That, and the lure of nearby Dublin, where they had unrationed delights you could not buy in England, such as nylon stockings. We drove to Dublin one day, and I can still remember my father commanding my mother to wind the exotic nylons round her midriff to conceal them from the eyes of the customs officer on the way back across the border. Exciting times.

Thus it was that on various summer holidays I found myself playing golf at Rosemont in Scotland, Sandwich in Kent, Troon in Scotland, somewhere in Devon whose name escapes me and somewhere else in Northern Ireland so remote I don't think it even had a name. Thus it was also that in due course I found myself sent away to school in Scotland, four hundred miles from home. I always thought at the time that I was sent there because my father had gone there (and his had, too) and he didn't see why I should avoid the horror of it, but I now think it may have been because the school had its own golf course, and he was enjoying it vicariously through me. The school was called Glenalmond, and the only famous person who ever emerged from it was the comic actor Robbie Coltrane, who on Desert Island Discs early in 1992 described the school as a terrible place to be, and as the 'Eton of the North'. It was nothing of the sort. It was the Parkhurst of the North, an open prison so far from civilisation that nobody could run away even if they wanted to.

Being a Scottish school, it gave golf a higher priority than other sports and had its own nine-hole course at a time when it had no swimming pool. (It had a rushy, rocky river, into which a friend of mine once dived and came up with blood pouring from his face. He had broken his nose on a rock at the bottom – and this, mark you, was in the approved bathing place. Exciting times.) The course was a tough one, being carved out of heather, rushes, rabbit droppings and that green stuff which is officially described as grass but is more like a kind of non-stick moss. It was challenging, and drew many of the boys to it on Sunday, which was the golf-playing day. Some of the boys, like me, were drawn to play. Others were drawn to look for lost golf balls and sell them at a profit to the players. The latter class were mostly drawn from the more

Calvinistic among the Scottish students, who were firmly convinced that playing golf on the Sabbath was wicked but that
collecting golf balls for sale at a profit was not.

It is one of the stranger memories of my schooldays, striding on
to a tee on this wild, Wordsworthian golf course with the hills
lowering in all directions, to see no sign of life anywhere except
for these God-fearing fellow pupils wandering purposefully
through the rough, or tramping along the burn that ran down the
middle of the course, like gold prospectors looking for the big one.
It was even worse when these black vultures were gathered round
the green you were aiming at, as you were convinced that by
the time you got there your ball would have vanished into their
capacious pockets. One of the more shameless ones once told me
that he had not seen my ball arrive, but that he was prepared to
sell it back to me for five bob. Ever since then I have had a deep
distrust of organised religion.

(So, interestingly, has Robbie Coltrane. When asked by Sue
Lawley what other book he wanted on his desert island beside the
Bible and Shakespeare, his immediate reaction was to ask if he was
really obliged to take the Bible. A rather dull book, he said . . .)

I think I was really quite good by the time I left school. Especially
round the green. My long play used to suffer now and then with
mysterious slices, but my chipping and putting was usually pretty
reliable. This was because my father had also converted the garden
at home into a nine-hole golf course. None of the holes was more
than thirty yards, some only ten yards, but they were all challenging holes, usually round trees or over rose beds. When you have
to chip over a flower bed and make the ball stop dead the other
side, you begin to work out the mechanics of lofted iron play. It
stood me in good stead in real-life golf, though people watching
me line up a tricky eight-iron shot and take some time over it
never realised that I was trying to visualise, in my mind's eye, a
large rose bush between me and the pin, so that I could chip over
it. I can also remember inventing a shot of my own, which was
done almost entirely with the wrists (I don't think the arms moved
at all) to impart a huge back spin to a short shot so that it would
not go into the gravel path just beyond the second hole . . .

My father used also to buy large quantities of books about golf, which I found totally useless. They were usually called *Play Power Golf* or *Improve Your Golf Out of all Recognition* and were signed by famous golfers though not, I now realise, written by them. They all seemed to feature black and white photographs of the author playing perfect shots, or, even worse, exploded diagrams of the human body showing *which* muscle came into play at *what* point during the final downswing. I could never hit a golf ball for a week after seeing one of those dreadful diagrams. These books never seemed remotely to approach the real world of sliced tee shots and missed putts. If only they had been full of black and white photos captioned 'Here is me, hitting another wild slice into the rough at the Open,' I might have been more encouraged than I was by seeing the muscle structures of people called Hagan and Hogan.

Still, I'm glad he took me to see some of the great players at work. There were no championship courses in Wales that I was aware of, but we were within motoring distance of Hoylake, Birkdale and so on, so he would sometimes drag me off for the day, which is how I came to see Gary Player, Bobby Locke, Max Faulkner, Dai Rees and others in action. Or at least to see them through the thousands of spectators who spent their whole time running up and down sand dunes to get there first. The one golfer I remember very clearly was Christy O'Connor, who always seemed attended by four or five Irish priests. Why, I asked my father, was it necessary to have so many priests in attendance on one golfer?

'He hasn't asked them to be here,' said my father, who was as anti-religion as me or Robbie Coltrane. 'They are probably betting on him to win, knowing the Irish, and they are keeping a close eye on their investment.'

So at the age of eighteen or nineteen I was a good, quite experienced golfer, well versed in the history of the game. And I gave it up. Mostly, I suppose, because I then moved to London, in Notting Hill, which is light years from the nearest golf course. But more than that it was because my father no longer lived with me, and was not there to motivate me. I took my golf clubs with me and they lay in a store room, sad and rusting, until they were stolen during a burglary. After that my memory of the game gradually faded, although I hope it is true that your swing never really leaves you, like your ability to ride a bicycle. (If it ever comes back again, I fear it will come back again with my old slice, though.) My father died ten years ago. The other day my step-mother rang me up from North Wales.

'Miles, your father's golf clubs have surfaced in the garage. They're a very good set. Won't you come and take them away? Then you could start playing again.'

My God. It's my father, motivating me from beyond the grave. And I know that deep down I really want to start again, because I can remember how nice it was walking through a lovely landscape swinging a club, and I can't remember how awful it was hitting a shot badly that you thought you had mastered, or making a mess of a putt just when you were about to birdie the hole . . . I also want to confirm my memory that my father had one left-handed club, which he kept in his bag for those rare occasions when you can't get at a lie right-handed – he was in fact left-handed but had been forced by unbending parents to become right-handed. So it looks as if in the next year or so I shall start playing again, as long as I can get over my fear of having my ball stolen by God-fearing Scotsmen in the rough. The other day I caught myself staring out of the window at my present garden, idly converting it in my mind's eye to a small nine-hole pitch and putt course. It looks as if the child really is father to the man. The person I feel sorry for in all this is, no, not my wife, but my four-year-old son, who may find himself one day having golf lessons merely because I need someone to play against. So does history repeat itself.

A GALLERY OF THE GREAT

Peter Alliss

It has indeed been a privilege for me to have been involved with the game of golf all of my life. Fortunately, my father was one of the noble breed of professionals around in the embryonic days of golf when things were moving at an alarming rate.

The great boom came between 1910 and 1940, despite the fact that we had the Great War, world recession and Hitler looming on the horizon. But it was during that time that most golf courses were built, golf professionals from Great Britain, particularly Scotland, moved westwards and the game spread like wildfire through the United States and indeed all other parts of the world, particularly where the British Colonial service opened up new routes for trade and industry and, as the various Embassies were allocated, golf courses sprang up. I often sit ruminating on days gone by and am slightly saddened by the fact that the vast majority of modern-day professionals don't seem to have concern or indeed care about the past . . . they have no feel for it. Of course, a few do – the Americans Tom Watson and Ben Crenshaw for example; but the majority are only interested in the game to produce as much money as they can as quickly as possible.

Looking back over the history of golf, it has always intrigued me that nobody really knows when or where it started. Of course Scotland is looked upon by most as being the home of golf. But what about Holland? Early pictures there depict players from the 15th and 16th centuries busily playing a game that looks uncommonly like golf, albeit played through the winter on sheets of ice! Scotland or Holland – I wonder which. Your ideas are suddenly thrown right out of gear by looking at old drawings or sculptures from pre-historic caves depicting figures knocking a circular object about with a stick. Could that have been a form of golf?

The earliest golf as far as Scotland is concerned was predominantly on the east coast, although Prestwick in Ayrshire staged the first playing of the Open Championship. In those far-off days much of the golf was played by the wealthy merchants and landowners of the day and many belonged to the union of Masons. The Grand Masonic Order being rather secretive, early records of matches, games and challenges are very scarce indeed. In fact we are led to believe that the first thirty or forty years of golfing records at the Honourable Company of Edinburgh Golfers' wonderful golf course at Gullane (which staged the 1992 Open Championship) were destroyed because *they* didn't want others to know of their matches who won and lost, how much money changed hands and who had the most port wine on that particular day.

I must confess I'd like to have been there, certainly to watch James Braid, J. H. Taylor and Harry Vardon in their heyday. How wonderful it must have been to see three very different styles marching down totally unmanicured fairways, using very strange-looking equipment but scoring amazingly well: Vardon bringing his very special elegant brand of golf to the attention of the public; J. H. Taylor more a man for the broadsword than the rapier; and the tall, rather sombre-looking Scot, James Braid, who was perhaps a mixture of them both. My father, Percy Alliss, always told me how fortunate he had been to play golf with Vardon, albeit when he was perhaps past his best – he was certainly nearer fifty than forty. He was immediately struck by Vardon's balance, timing and how with the minimum of effort he could sweep the ball away astonishing distances.

Yes, that would have been interesting indeed . . . but then how would they have compared to Walter Hagen and Gene Sarazen who were to take much of the American continent by storm when Vardon, Braid and Taylor had become too old to travel. Hagen was the first of the great showmen, flamboyant, good-looking. Stories of him are legion: a man who liked the ladies, a huge drinker, who smoked forty cigarettes a day . . . immaculate clothes for every occasion. Again I'm quoting from my father's memories of him; in fact he wasn't really like that at all. Oh yes, he liked the look of a well turned ankle and did smoke cigarettes but never drank as much as people thought. He never said no to a drink, that was his great gift. He would airily take a 'whatever' when offered and then slip it behind the aspidistra or pour it into a nearby vase. For there was no way Hagen could have kept up his brilliant performance on the golf course if he'd gone to bed every night the worse for drink and woken up in the morning with a hangover.

How I would love to have seen him play, particularly in 1931 – the year I was born. That year my father, who was working in Germany and not eligible to play in the Ryder Cup team, had gone to America to report for the Daily Express and entered for the Canadian Open Championship. Lo and behold, he and Hagen tied, so, after seventy-two holes off they went for a thirty-six hole play-off. Believe it or not, at the end of that thirty-six holes they were still tied. So, sudden death . . . Hagen winning at the first extra hole. I'd like to have seen that.

I'd also have liked to have seen the great battles that Hagen had with Sarazen, the Jack Russell or corgi of the golfing world, only 5′5″, stocky, of Italian descent, aggressive and with a rather crude swing compared with Hagen, who it must be said was not as elegant a swinger of the club as Vardon; but he had something . . . not least a most wonderful temperament and a putting touch second to none. Arguably the greatest player of all time was around on those occasions: Bobby Jones, the amateur from Atlanta, Georgia. When you look at Jones's record it's perhaps the most extraordinary and brilliant in the whole history of golf. He played his entire life internationally as an amateur. He won the Open Championship of America and the Amateur Championship and the Open and Amateur Championship of Great Britain. All four titles in one year, hence the growth of the fabled grand slam. He only played in about twenty-five or twenty-six major championships, and won thirteen of them, so his strike rate for victories was almost 50 per cent. An extraordinary man, again using hickory shafted clubs, golf balls that were ever improving but nowhere near as consistent as the ones used today.

Bobby Jones was the great ambassador of the game. He retired when he was thirty, immediately turned professional and went into the business of making instructional golf films, which can be bought today – for quite large sums of money – on video. So the name of Jones lives on. Jones and a friend named Clifford Roberts were the instigators of the Augusta National Golf Club where the Masters has been played every year since the early thirties. I would love to have seen him play in his heyday. It was very sad to meet him in the early fifties when his body was already being racked by rheumatoid arthritis. How sad it was to see this wonderfully elegant man slowly become a twisted wreck. Death indeed was a happy release for Bobby Jones, though utterly unfair for a man who had given the world of golf so much.

Henry Cotton was emerging by the early thirties. My father was then in his mid-thirties, some fifteen or sixteen years older than Cotton, but in fact they had many good battles. Cotton was always very complimentary about my father, his approach to the game, his swing, his easy rhythm and his simplicity. I'd like to have seen Cotton in those early days, winning his first Championship in 1934 against the whole might of the American Ryder Cup team, in pouring rain at Carnoustie. How would he compare with today's great stars? How many hours did he practise? Was the lady in his life – Mrs Moss – really a member of the Fray Bentos meat packing company from Argentina? Ah, Toots, what a formidable partnership they were! I was privileged to spend a lot of time with them, for Henry gave youngsters very sound advice on many aspects of golf if they were prepared to listen. Ah, Cotton and Jones, Hagen and Sarazen . . .

But what of the next emerging breed? There are so many of them that it is difficult to mention them all, but in my book *perhaps* the greatest player of all was Byron Nelson. Here is a man who won eleven tournaments in a row, then had a break for a couple of weeks and won three or four more before the season ended. His efforts were rather pooh-poohed at the time because it was the War years and most of the great players were away serving their President and Country. Nelson was a haemophiliac, and so exempt from War service, but he played a lot of Red Cross matches, and it was during these tournaments that he set up extra-ordinary scoring records. Imagine going a whole year – fifty years ago, with the equipment of the day – averaging just over sixty-eight shots per round. It's easy enough to say the opposition was thin on the ground but even if you go out on your own with a marker, a score card and a pencil you still have to physically 'do it', and you still can become 'afraid' when you are scoring well and talk yourself into mistakes and failure. Nelson never did. He, like Jones, retired early, but I'm still tempted to say he was the greatest.

He certainly was for a time; and I think it totally unfair to say he had nobody to play against, because there were Snead, Hogan, Demaret and a host of other stars all able to play for certain times during the early forties. Snead and Hogan, indeed, were next on the scene. According to Peter Thomson, Hogan was the finest striker and greatest strategist the game of golf has ever seen. Not many people would argue that his record is unique, although he was a late starter and was in his thirties before he started winning. In his early days he had a wild swing and big hook, and it looked as though he, like many others before, was destined not to make it. Then, suddenly, he found a 'secret'. Off he went; and he dominated American professional golf in the late forties and through the fifties – even surviving a horrific car smash when he was in a head-on collision with a bus in dense fog. He battled back to health, although the circulation in his legs was never quite the same, to win championships again and captain the Ryder Cup team.

Hogan was a quiet man, very aware he had little formal education: he didn't go to college like most, if not all the players of the United States today. But for me he had an elegance and aura about him that is given to very few. When Hogan spoke, people listened.

Sam Snead – there's a man for you. He would be in my twenty-five top athletes of the 1900s. He was still winning tournaments on the professional circuit in his mid-fifties, and he gave up counting the times he went round a golf course in less than his age after the thousandth time. Even now, despite failing eyesight and being well into his eighties, he still has a fluency about his walk and style that makes you stand back, look and marvel. That wonderful

Connery-007 walk, the rakish straw hats that were so much his hallmark. Oh yes, just imagine a four ball with any of those.

Now we tiptoe towards different generations. Bobby Locke from South Africa was the most unusual-looking golfer I have ever seen: a man with entirely his own style of play, the best chipper and putter I have ever seen in my life. A wonderful golfing philosopher, a traveller and a genius. He would be in my top ten players of all time, along with Peter Thomson the young Australian who learnt so much from Locke but refused to admit it. He had the easiest of all swings, and the most clinical of golfing brains. I can still remember seeing him for the first time. It was June 15th, 1951. I was home after completing my two years' National Service with the RAF Regiment, and the Festival of Britain Tournament was being played at Bournemouth on the Queens Park Golf Course, a beautiful municipal golf course sadly altered by the intrusion of a dual-carriageway. The professional was Don Curtis, a friend of my father, who said he was one of the most beautiful players he'd ever seen. He was a somewhat introverted man who, after completing his War service felt that he was playing less well than he had before, and gave up the professional circuit to concentrate on running the Golf Club at Queens Park and giving lessons. I stood on the veranda of the old wooden clubhouse (later knocked down to make way for a roundabout) and watched the young Thomson, in white shoes, dark green trousers, white short-sleeved shirt and white floppy hat, putting out on the final green using an old Braid Mills putter with a hickory shaft, then jauntily raising the floppy hat to the crowd and moving away. Everyone was saying he was destined for stardom, and how right they were: for three years later he won his first Open Championship at Royal Birkdale. He was to go on to win three in a row and complete perhaps his greatest victory in 1965 when he was no longer considered a threat to the mighty Americans who were here in great numbers but he triumphed and accepted victory with his usual slightly sardonic tongue in cheek smiling attitude.

Gary Player, too, learned much from Bobby Locke. Being South African you had an awful long way to go if you were going to make your mark in golf: Johannesburg to London, London to

New York in the days of the old Constellations and Stratocruisers. Seat no. 7 was always Bobby Locke's – first class of course. It was a single, and he always belted himself in as tight as he possibly could. It was the only way to travel, he reckoned. He should have known: he was a war-time flier, ferrying Liberators across the Atlantic from Canada to the UK and also taking part in the Middle Eastern campaign.

Max Faulkner, Dai Rees, Charlie Ward, Fred Daly, Harry Bradshaw were all wonderful homegrown talents who had great skills and character. I remember Fred Daly winning the Championship at Hoylake in 1947 – yes, I was there: it was the first Open Championship I ever went to; and then Max Faulkner winning in 1951 at Portrush in Northern Ireland – the only time the Championship has been played in that country. I'd like to think it won't be the only one.

The sixties and the emergence of Arnold Palmer – what a swashbuckling style *he* had. Nobody had ever seen anything like Arnold except those old enough to remember Walter Hagen. There's something of Hagen in Palmer. He was the people's champion. He went into the rough, he missed shots, he smoked incessantly, he hitched up his trousers, he glared around, and he had arms like Popeye! He was a new American hero. Another one was to come along very soon in the unlikely shape of Jack Nicklaus, 5′10″ and pudgy (one hesitates to say fat), with an unattractive crew-cut hairstyle, who in the space of a few years usurped Palmer's throne, let his hair grow two or three inches, lost thirty pounds and became the Golden Bear, the darling of American golf. Nicklaus' record tells us that in the statistical sense, at least, he must be the greatest of them all. After thirty years of virtually uninterrupted golf as amateur and professional – I don't think his record will ever be equalled.

Perhaps I glossed too quickly over Gary Player. He's one of the few players to have won the four major titles, the US PGA, American Open, The Masters and our own Open Championship, a fiercely competitive man with a sense of humour all his own, he continually amazes me by his undying, unflagging interest and love of competitive golf.

Speaking of the old commonwealth we can't go by without mentioning the only real class left-handed player in my lifetime on the professional scene – Bob Charles. A new recipient of the CBE for services to golf, I remember him fondly. He was always the smartest dresser on the golf course, even if his taste tended to the sombre, featuring immaculate dark grey slacks with a razor edge crease, black shoes you could see yourself to shave in, black socks that might even be cashmere, a beautifully ironed shirt, lighter grey sweater: the personification of quiet elegance.

Next to Arnold Palmer, Seve Ballesteros is the most exciting player *I* have ever seen. Those dashing good looks, hair as black as a raven's wing, carving and cutting his way around and out of trouble, holing monstrous putts, doing seemingly silly things, throwing tournaments away and snatching them back again – a joy to watch.

Ian Woosnam from Wales is another pleasantly exciting golfer to watch, and then there are Nick Faldo and Sandy Lyle, whose careers seem to have gone pretty well along parallel lines. First it was Sandy Lyle winning an event of importance then it was Faldo, then Lyle then Faldo, back and forward until suddenly Lyle in the late eighties totally lost his form, while Faldo equally suddenly seemed to find a magic formula which would allow him never to hit another crooked shot in his life. The magic of David Leadbetter and the persistence and desire of Nick Faldo, they made a formidable pair as teacher and pupil. Still, it wasn't quite as easy as some might have thought. Faldo still missed fairways, went out of bounds, three-putted, didn't chip close enough; yet what a wonderful spell he enjoyed over a few years, winning the US Masters and the British Open Championship twice each, and thereby pushing Sandy Lyle a fair way into the background.

The list could go on and on. Depending on my mood – who would I really say was best? – you have to give me two or three bites of the cherry – I would like to have seen the old boys – Braid, Taylor, Vardon together and making up the fourball; perhaps Arnaud Massey the only Frenchman ever to win our Open Championship. Certainly, Hagen, Sarazen, Percy Alliss and Henry Cotton, that would have been a joy. Then Snead, Hogan and

Nelson: could there ever have been a better three than them? Who to make up the four . . . I'm going to be a bit selfish and think I'd like to have slipped in there, I'm not sure which one I would have chosen as a partner . . . I'm sure any would have carried me through . . . on and on to many of the players I have had the privilege of watching many times or indeed competing and playing with . . . Ballesteros and Woosnam are a delight to watch, entirely different to the slightly mechanical movements of Faldo and Lyle . . . so much to see, so many lovely players to watch: and no, I've not forgotten two of the best: Lee Trevino and Tom Watson, the latter brisk and bright, Lee Trevino a pure genius. What a dream after a spell of the golf being reduced by the theorist whereby everything was done with dead wrists and strong legs. Watson brought a refreshing briskness and charm back to the game. He actually used his hands à la Henry Cotton, brisk and bright, swish the ball away, never seemingly ever missing a putt from six feet and in, winner of five of our own Championships, The Masters and so many other great events. It's difficult just to go by the hard facts and record books. From them Jack Nicklaus must reign supreme. Palmer, Player and Jacklin, Nicklaus – the big four – I just wish Arnold had perhaps been ten years younger and Jack three years younger and they'd all have been at their best together . . . what a joy that would have been!

All I know is that I have been blessed and privileged to have seen many of them and I hope there'll be some more in the years ahead . . . golf may be a rather strange, pedestrian old game but it is for me the mirror of life and as Henry Longhurst always said, it does manage to take us to so many beautiful places.

PREMIER LEAGUE

Ian Wallace

The elderly professional wore a mackintosh and muffler against the biting winds of East Anglia, and, as I addressed the ball with my juvenile-size hickory-shafted driver, he exhorted me to grip the ground inside my shoes like a parrot on its perch. I was all of eleven and we had come to Frinton-on-Sea for the Easter holidays. His unlikely tip worked, but only when he was there, like so many nostrums devised to unravel the mysteries of this maddening and utterly fascinating game.

I came to golf early because my father, a Fifer, played for much of his adult life to a handicap of eight – something to which I never aspired – and he just assumed that I would want to play and that I might as well start young. I wasn't born until he was fifty-one, so my childhood witnessed him gently declining from this pinnacle of excellence, but he remained a useful player into his seventies. As a captain of industry and Member of Parliament, he was able to afford holidays for my mother and myself at such exciting places as St Andrews, where another elderly professional called Davie Ayton, a man with piercing blue eyes and beautifully cut plus-fours, gave me more conventional tuition, with no ornithological similes.

Those St Andrews holidays in the early thirties could have put me off golf for life. Thankfully they whetted my appetite instead. While my father and mother played in splendour on the R & A or the New, our chauffeur Mackenzie and I were consigned to the then terrible, now vastly improved, Jubilee Course (sixpence a round, old money). I had a few clubs in a canvas bag purchased individually after great deliberation from Forgans. Mackenzie had an old bagful of my father's rejects. Such a person as Mackenzie sounds now quite absurdly feudal, but not in those times. I was devoted to him and, blind leading the blind, I had to teach him how to play.

He had served in the army in World War I and told me that his first contact with this historic game had been when he was detailed to caddy for one of the officers in a match in some eastern country. When he asked the sergeant major what golf was he received the terse reply, 'Golf, my lad, is 'ockey at the 'alt.'

Our early games together would have been acutely embarrassing on any normal golf course, but many of the other players were equally inept, and wildly off-course golf balls occasionally whined over our heads like bullets. Mackenzie compared it with some campaign he'd fought under General Allenby. The whole game was punctuated by urgent cries of 'Fore!' or even 'Look out!' but we gradually improved. In fact it was a marvellous place to learn the rudiments. Would that there were more such courses today where beginners could cut their teeth without infuriating the membership.

You may be wondering what all this has to do with the title of my story. Without those hazardous rounds with Mackenzie and the odd refresher lesson from Davie Ayton, I would never have been ready by 1935 for the big test when it came. I would never have been selected (ahead of my mother, for which she never forgave me) to play in one of the historic four-ball matches of the pre-war years.

In 1934 my parents decided to go further north for the annual holiday, to Spey Bay in Morayshire. St Andrews was a little too near my father's Fife constituency, and he wearied of being button-holed by disaffected constituents between the 18th green and the Grand Hotel (now a university hall of residence). He was a kind, caring man, but he needed a holiday like anyone else.

Though my father was what was then known as a National Liberal, he had a great respect for Ramsay MacDonald, who was uneasily presiding over a National Government. Ramsay was spending the holiday at Lossiemouth, his birthplace, where there is a beautiful golf course, which, alas, was not available to the golf-loving Prime Minister. He had been refused membership because of his pacifist views in World War I, and though it was offered again when he became Prime Minister, he felt unable to accept.

My father decided to invite him over for a game at Spey Bay. I have been fortunate for a player whose prowess never rose more than one notch above a hacker, to taste the delights of the R & A, Muirfield, Gleneagles, Troon, Old Prestwick, Wentworth and Royal St George's, Sandwich, but the course I go round in order to woo sleep, the one that is my true love, is Spey Bay.

Only a few hundred yards down the road from the course the river Spey completes its headlong dash to the sea. The village is tiny and the little railway station, then a useful feature, was to be an early Beeching casualty. At the time of this golf match the focus of the village was a hotel to which the same families returned year after year. About twenty years after this story it was burnt to the ground and a huge chunk of my memories went with it. But I digress.

The course itself, protected from the sea by a shingle bank, stretches from Spey Bay nearly to the fishing village of Port Gordon with the distant town of Buckie and the 900-foot Cullen Bin to make the view more interesting. The fairways are mostly closely-cropped heather, the rough a ferocious mixture of whins, bracken and high waving grass. The greens were usually covered with rabbit droppings. It was not a long course: the 'long' 16th was only 440 yards, and when at the 11th you turned for home with the sea on your right there was a cheerful profusion of sea pinks on the edge of the fairway. I write of it as it was over fifty years ago.

At breakfast on the day of the Prime Minister's visit my father turned to my mother and said, 'May, I really don't think you should play this morning. If you get into that rough you'll never get out, and we can't have the Prime Minister standing about waiting. I think Ian had better partner Peggie against Ramsay and myself.' This was a heavy blow for my mother, who was a keen golfer, but one who never managed to get a lower handicap than 19, to which, it has to be said, she seldom played. Peggie was her unmarried sister who was holidaying with us, and she was a very good golfer indeed, playing off 6. I had no handicap but could certainly beat my mother, a point of honour with any sixteen-year-old.

My mother took it very well, but I could tell it rankled. Auntie had a beautiful soprano voice and was a good pianist. My mother could match neither of those talents, so there was also a whiff of sisterly jealousy in the air but I had neither the maturity nor the inclination to stand down in her favour.

The large black government limousine scrunched through the gravel up to the hotel and a detective jumped out to open the door for Ramsay, the only other occupant apart from the chauffeur and a West Highland terrier. Ramsay was wearing a tweed jacket, waistcoat and knickerbockers with heavy woollen stockings and stout brogues. He gravely greeted us, though it was hard to see his eyes through his thick, horn-rimmed glasses. The detective, a tall man, wore a grey pin-stripe suit and a brown homburg, an incongruous outfit for the wilds of Morayshire. If you are thinking that I have a photographic memory, you'd be right. I snapped the scene with my Kodak No. 2 Brownie and have the print to this day.

My father was on edge and had been since he got up. He was highly strung and desperately wanted the morning to be a success. We made our way to the first tee where there was a larger crowd of caddies than usual. These were mostly fishermen's sons who'd walked the mile or so from Port Gordon to earn half a crown for a morning's work.

The detective unloaded Ramsay's golf bag and there was a concerted rush towards him led by Hamish, the only grown man in the group, who seized the bag with a triumphant grin and carried it towards the tee. There was a groan of disappointment from the others. 'No, not you,' said my father. 'Oh yes,' said Ramsay, 'let him keep it.'

I learned many years later that Hamish, which is not his real name, had survived a severe attack of meningitis as a boy, and it had left him slightly handicapped. Despite the heat of the day he wore a serge suit with the sleeves folded back so that from the elbow to the shoulder the lining was displayed. His face was the colour of mahogany, he was missing several front teeth, his eyes were light blue and he very rarely spoke. Caddying was his only chance of employment. Ramsay, more relaxed than my father, had clearly taken in that whole situation at first glance. Then, turning to the detective he said, 'You'd better take the dog for a walk and meet us here later.' There was no question of his acting as a bodyguard on the course.

Auntie Peggie and I shared a fatal weakness, which should have ruled us out of this contest altogether. We were compulsive gigglers, amused by the same sort of absurdities. When Hamish stepped forward to tee up the Prime Minister's ball, he pressed in the peg at an angle of nearly forty-five degrees to the ground and the ball fell off. My father glared at Auntie and me, aware of our track record, daring us to make any sort of sound. Eventually Hamish got it straight and the match began.

I cannot recall much of what happened that morning except that we were evenly matched and at the 2nd I whispered to my caddy, a boy of about my own age called Sandy, that he should tee up for Ramsay rather than Hamish. I was only allowed a caddy if I was playing with my father, who hated looking for my ball if it went astray. He was a dear man, but becoming irritable with advancing years.

That impatience showed when Ramsay disappeared into deep rough at the 9th after one of his rare shots that was not on line. 'Why doesn't he send in his caddy to pick it up and then we can get on?' muttered my father. Instead Ramsay, after a five-minute search, straddled a gorse bush and dealt it a surprisingly violent blow. The ball sailed out of the rough and ended up six feet from the pin, a hell of a shot for a sixty-nine-year-old, which denied my father, a mere sixty-seven, the satisfaction of winning the hole for his side, as Auntie and I had each played one more. 'Not bad, John, eh?' said Ramsay, one of the few remarks he made on the round.

At the 14th tee Hamish, frustrated at being denied the honour of teeing up his famous employer's ball all morning, suddenly snatched it from Sandy and stabbed it and a peg into the ground at an angle that gave the ball a tremendous task to defy the laws

of gravity. It remained on the peg. We looked at it unbelievingly. Had he rubbed it with glue? The Premier and First Lord of the Treasury addressed it for several seconds and began his slow back swing. Just as he reached the top, the ball could stand the strain no longer and fell off.

Auntie and I exploded with laughter. The whole morning had been a great strain. Hamish and the other caddies joined in but Ramsay and my father did not. 'Stop laughing and tee up the Prime Minister's ball,' yelled my father more or less in my direction. I rushed forward, so did Auntie, so did Hamish and we all collided heavily at Ramsay's feet. We lay for a few moments in the grip of hysteria made worse by Ramsay regarding us from above without the flicker of a smile.

Eventually order was restored and I managed to sober up enough to tee his ball myself. 'Thank you,' said our leader in his mellow baritone voice. Despite all the distractions and the distinct possibility of Auntie or I disgracing ourselves a second time, he hit the ball straight up the middle as usual.

When we finished our round we were met by the detective whose crestfallen look made us wonder if he was the bearer of bad news. He certainly was. 'I'm sorry, sir,' he mumbled, 'but I've lost the dog.' Ramsay looked at us and for the first time that morning he smiled. 'Well, well,' he said, 'this is the man who is supposed to guard the Prime Minister, and he can't even look after a wee dog.'

My mother died fifty years later at the age of ninety-four. She had been a widow for nearly forty years. Conversing with her latterly involved switches from well-remembered events of her younger days to charming fantasies. One day when we were talking about something quite different she suddenly said, 'Do you remember those holidays we had at Spey Bay before the war?' 'Of course,' I replied. 'You probably never realised it,' she went on, 'but Ramsay MacDonald used to hang about outside the hotel every morning hoping I'd play golf with him. But I never did.'

I should have refused to play that August morning in 1935. She wouldn't have giggled at Hamish.

PLAYING TO
YOUR HANDICAP

Donald Soper

Religion and golf are in many respects different varieties of human experience but as a professional in the practice of the one and an amateur in the practice of the other, I have found that what happens on a golf course has a great deal in common with what happens in church. In their various ways I have been committed to both activities (imperfectly of course) and my experience in these two fields has often seemed more than complementary, even identical. In the same way that the Old Testament is a storehouse of comment on the prospects of obeying the injunctions in the New Testament, so the golf course has provided authoritative comment on the prospect of conducting the good life. There is much in the Rules of Golf that belongs equally naturally to the Laws of the Pentateuch, and much funnier into the bargain.

Golf is a revelation, or worse still a disclosure, of human weakness. As a round of golf is a more personal and individual activity than a soccer match, so it calls forth personal reactions that have marked resemblances to the doctrine of original sin. 'Is my friend in the bunker or is the rotter on the green?' is an appropriate text for this moral fault. I wonder how often the second shot at a particular hole is played with a ball that has dropped conveniently on the fairway from a hole in a trouser pocket, rather than the true one which has careered off into the rough. Have you, gentle reader, never nudged the ball into a more favourable lie? I have. Indeed as a parson I have sometimes comforted myself with the reflection that playing golf on a Sunday morning rather than attending matins may promote a more penitential attitude at evensong.

The more I ponder on this moral theme the clearer comes the

realisation of the identity of approach to the practice alike of good golf and the good life. The key word in golf is 'handicap'. The key word in religion is 'sin'. They represent in their respective spheres that perfection is out of the question. We do not start from scratch and even if we play to scratch we have not attained the perfect round. Our human behaviour is also handicapped just as is our proficiency on the golf course. We may indulge our dreams of perfection but they are a snare and a delusion if we believe them. Nevertheless, the question 'What is your handicap?' can be much too clearly specified on the golf course when we use the word 'handicap' to quantify our ability to deal with it. It is much more difficult to quantify the moral handicap on the 'daily round and the common task', as the hymn puts it. What is common ground (or common bunker if you like) is the promotion of humility. We are all sinners 'saved by grace' perhaps but certainly not achieving a complete victory over original sin. We are golfers handicapped by ineradicable faults and falling short of a perfect score. Yet in both fields playing to your handicap can be both realistic and satisfying, even if you cannot play to scratch, let alone better than scratch. The good life and the good golf is like bringing both down to single figures. But how to apply this good intention is another matter.

At first sight, just as the Ten Commandments are a selection of ordinances set within a host of others, as a reading of the book of Deuteronomy will quickly reveal, so the rules of golf, both for the conduct of play and for the striking of the ball, are many and complicated. Disciples of both creeds may well agree with the great Sarah Bernhardt, who, when asked to express an opinion on the Ten Commandments, said there were too many of them. No wonder, then, that in both pursuits this often daunting accumulation of requirements has been pragmatically reduced to a single, all-embracing rule. In religion it is 'Love your neighbour'; in golf, 'Keep your eye on the ball'. What makes this injunction more difficult is that in the parable of the Good Samaritan your neighbour also happens to be your enemy. However, to keep to golf, the ethic of unremitting attention to the ball is a golden rule the significance of which can stretch far beyond the confines of a particular green. I have paid careful attention to golf courses. I know the geography of my local course intimately, for I have visited parts of it that few other players ever travel. I have received much instruction from many sources as to the means of propelling that small ball into a remote hole. Moreover, most of the time between holes I have no difficulty in keeping my eye on the ball after I have attempted to hit it.

Let me as a Methodist give my testimony. I think that over the years I have succeeded rather better in keeping the religious injunction than the golfing one. Try as I do, or strictly speaking, as an old man, try as I did, I found it well-nigh impossible to fix my eye on the ball at the moment of trying to hit it. Psychologists have told me that the present is invariably to some extent involved in the past and the future, and that therefore however strong our concentration on the fleeting instance of applying the club to the ball, some elements of the past, some anticipation of the future, will intrude. They may well be right, and if you, gentle reader, find any comfort in their analysis, you are most welcome to it. I might add that psychologists do not seem any better golfers than the rest of us.

There is nevertheless a lesson, which I am still in the process of learning, to be extracted from this process of keeping one's eye on the ball. It is this question of priority. There must be almost as many books written about how to hit a golf ball effectively as upon any comparable activity. What to do with your arms, where to put your feet, how to adjust your hips, how to align your nose over the ball, how to avoid the truncheon stroke, and the late cut and the pull and the slice and so on. Amid all this good advice, which in my case has only occasionally become good news, there is a fact as valuable in the realm of golf as in the wider world of daily living. It is that there are certain dispositions of the soul as well as of the body which if obeyed bring with them a kind of harmony. The injunction to seek first the Kingdom of God carries with it the promise that everything else necessary to that adventure will tend to fall into place. The injunction to keep your eye on the ball can be a practical example in the game of golf of 'first things first'. Look at the ball and your head will be more likely to keep still, your arms, legs and nose will take up their appropriate stations, and you will produce a more co-ordinated swing.

I confess that golf for me has at times been more like an addiction than a relaxation, and therefore it raises the question of priorities. Which comes first, preparing a sermon or practising your putting? If my first responsibility is to seek the Kingdom of God, to what extent does that kingdom include a place for the golf course? And what are the hours of play? Let me illustrate with a story, which you will agree is most pertinent in this question of priorities. A golfer was teeing up at a hole beside a road, at a critical stage of a critical match. As he addressed the ball, already 'wound up', his eye caught a funeral cortège passing by. Whereupon he put his club down, removed his hat, and stood silently until the cortège passed. This diversion destroyed his rhythm and he lost the match. In the clubroom afterwards his victorious fellow-golfer said how much he admired what had been done, and how well it reflected on the behaviour of his defeated rival – to which the defeated partner replied 'What else could I do? We'd been married for thirty years!' Golf can never be first in the hierarchy of us human beings, but when that priority is established it can be a contribution to the full life, and I believe that God will smile upon those who find this true relationship between work and play.

To mention God's smile is to recognise an element in religion which is so often undervalued in comparison with the place it holds in the world of golf. Is there any topic that attracts so much humour as golf? To the theologian the attributes of God are infinite wisdom and infinite love; but so many golf stories are irresistibly funny, and assume that if God is to be taken seriously, he must have an equally infinite sense of humour. I sometimes, in this wicked world, think that our only hope in our stupidity and our immorality is that God can laugh at our misdeeds as well as deplore them. I am sure God does not snigger or giggle, but I do like to think that he would enjoy what to me is the best golf story, and indeed the most perceptive.

A parson with time to spare on his way home from an appointment dropped into a golf clubhouse and asked if there was any

chance of a game, as by good fortune he had his clubs in the boot of his car. He was recommended to a member who was also looking for a game, but warned that this member was addicted to outbursts of blasphemy. 'Leave that to me,' said the parson, and they drove off. It was as he had been warned. Missing a short putt his companion ejaculated 'Oh, God, missed again!' When he repeated the blasphemous comment at the next two holes the parson could put up with it no longer. He warned the culprit that such blasphemy would not go unpunished, that he might, indeed, be struck down by a thunderbolt from on high. Undeterred, the fellow did the same thing at the next hole. Whereupon down came a thunderbolt, flattening the parson and leaving the blasphemer unsinged, followed promptly by an angelic voice from above, 'Oh, God, missed again!'

Beneath the humour of this story there lies for me a truth that belongs both to the world of religion and to that of golf. Perhaps for many in this secular age it will be more acceptable in the non-ecclesiastical frame of a game such as golf: golf is not finished at the 18th hole when the round is over. Life is not ended when our earthly lease runs out. If this is so, then the ultimate meaning of religion and golf is an unfolding experience both here and here-after, and that applies to God's children whether they are playing golf or not. If the game of life is an ongoing adventure I must believe that such an adventure will go on, and what is more that God will be increasingly involved in it. The mistakes that are inevitable in the play of the best golfers are not confined to a game on an earthly course. The angel Gabriel who yelled out 'Missed again!' was subject to the same ongoing limitations. I did not begin to write this essay as a sermon; but maybe golf can be a therapeutic exercise, and that need not impair its delights alike for the experts and for those like me who regard the immortal Sid Field as our guide, philosopher and friend. I can still hear him say in his hilari-ous sketch, when invited to put an old ball down after he had dismissed two new ones out of bounds, 'But I haven't got an old ball, they're all new.' God bless him. I wonder what his handicap is now.

FANTASTICAL

Jeremy Kemp

The adventures of A. A. Milne's famous characters Winnie the Pooh and the others often strike even very young readers as pretty fantastical. He never tells us if they played golf, but some of the chapter headings are mightily suggestive of the game: 'In which Piglet is entirely surrounded by water', or 'In which we are introduced to some bees . . .' and so on. I remember very well seeing a colleague, somewhat given to histrionics on the golf course, almost completely hidden by a bush, but apparently belabouring the ground with a six-iron and howling loudly. It turned out that he had good reason to howl, if not to belabour: his ball was lodged in a wasps' nest – more aggressive than bees, and less useful. We have heard of David Feherty's encounter with an adder in practice at Wentworth, and seen that alligator about to take a hand (literally) in a tournament in Florida. In Nuwara Eliyah, high in the tea country of Sri Lanka, I have myself observed genuine jungle encroaching on to the fairway, and always dreaded to wonder what it might have concealed – anything from tiger up to tiger down.

This unique course was negotiated with the aid of three caddies: one to carry your bag and not one but two 'forward caddies'. The duty of these was to keep your ball in play without apparently cheating. I often wondered if they kept secreted about their persons duplicates of every known make and number of golf ball, because in spite of some wildish driving and far too many blind shots, I never lost a single ball. I feel certain that speed of eye and sleight of hand was the answer, for their desperately poor station in life could not have permitted investment in a sack of spare golf balls. You don't get rich picking tea.

The map, or yardage card, here offers numerous warnings to a golfer, such as 'Floody Place', 'Big Stones and Rox', 'Rather Boggy and Sad', 'Sandy Pit' and 'Nice for Picnics' – members of links courses beware – all very Pooh-esque.

It's a truism to observe that that which lies firmly in the past (reading *Winnie the Pooh*, for instance) feels somehow richer, sweeter, softer, fuller, better. Nostalgia is a very powerful emotion. On the links, memory can make holed putts longer, fine drives even further, and bills quite emphatically smaller.

The year to which I revert is 1975. The time: early autumn. The place: Perthshire – the Gleneagles Hotel. The course: The King's. The contest: Great Britain versus USA. The handicap: 15.

I travelled north on the night express that was known in those days as the Royal Highlander, from Euston to Inverness. There is something about sleeping on a train that adds a tinge of romance; unfortunately this is much tarnished when one has to leave the train at 6.42 in the morning, with no Pullman car, no kippers – no breakfast of any kind. It must be a pure privilege that the trains stop at Auchterarder at all. It comprises about 20 cottages and five distilleries. I took a taxi to the hotel, and was very impressed. It was the kind of hotel where if you are seen carrying a small parcel across the foyer three uniformed flunkeys immediately pounce upon you, seize your parcel and carry it with great importance to the concierge's desk about four paces away. This service was estimated to be worth ten bob, at least.

The following day I had a wrestling match with an eager helper. I had set out from the hotel carrying my golf bag (seven irons and a putter only) en route for the pro's shop, about three minutes' leisurely stroll. Almost at once the bag was seized from behind. 'I'll take that one for you now, sir,' came a voice. There was a brief tug-o'-war, which I immediately lost. You need to be accustomed to that brand of olden days' service; if you're not you are in grave danger of feeling mildly foolish, if not downright embarrassed as you eagerly pursue your escorted parcel across the foyer. The staff were amazingly polite and wonderfully efficient, and the chef was no slouch, either. The setting was delightful. I can thoroughly recommend the place to anyone with a large private income or a recording contract with the Rolling Stones. In those days, I believe it still belonged to British Rail and you could just drive up, pay a green fee and enjoy your golf. Alas, no more.

However, showered and changed, shaved and manicured, I was now ready to keep my appointment with the late, great Henry Longhurst. At 10.20 exactly I was ushered into the presence, noticing as I went through the door a discreet sign: 'Hospitality'. In the centre of the room I immediately saw Henry Longhurst, completely encircled by cronies. He was shorter than I had expected, and immaculately dressed in a brown double-breasted suit. Someone murmured 'Henry' as I awaited my introduction to the great man.

'Henry,' the someone repeated slightly louder. 'Here's another of those idiots come up to have a go.'

'Jolly good,' said the great man. I shook his hand and offered a polite 'Good morning, Mr Longhurst. How are you today?'

He stared straight at me for a long pause – indeed, an endless pause – while I wondered what could possibly have been wrong with a polite 'Good morning, Mr Longhurst. How are you today?' Eventually, after a still longer pause, there came a subterranean rumble, and the deep, gruff but kindly voice finally issued from the depths of his chest. 'I am fighting a battle,' he announced, 'against drinking gin before luncheon . . . and I am happy to say that I am losing.' And dead on cue he produced from behind his back a pink gin, or something of the sort, that would have poleaxed a thirsty submariner. First impressions were of a dignified man, a gracious man, a dapper, mildly dandyish man with a potent sense of humour lurking not far beneath the surface. 'You know what?' he continued. 'I think the average chap at home would feel a lot better if he knew why you chaps were supposed to be celebrated . . . before each match they should show a piece of film in which you appeared prominently. The other week,' he said, 'there was a fellow here called Efrem Zimbalist Junior – and who the *fuck* has heard of him?' (Zimbalist was at this time probably appearing on television all round the world as frequently as any actor, or more so.) All this was delivered in that inimitable voice known to millions on two continents. I resisted the temptation to join him in his unequal struggle with gin before luncheon.

At this moment I received a message from Christopher Lee (who the fuck has heard of him?) saying that he hadn't touched a club for months and was desperate to get out for a few holes. I wondered how many months. I knew his handicap was three and that he was therefore out of my class. But worse was yet to come. On the first tee we were approached by an unknown man. Would we, he asked, gesturing vaguely at his friend, mind making up a four? The friend was well over six feet, spare, lean and vaguely familiar. It turned out that he was none other than the Open Champion, Tom Weiskopf, the victor of Troon.

I was ready to make a bolt for it, but somehow we agreed to play. 'Tom will want a bit on it, you know,' said the unknown man, who turned out to be Weiskopf's agent. 'What does he call "a bit"?' I asked suspiciously. This adventure, already far past the fanciful and fast approaching the fantastical, was now manifesting unpleasant signs of becoming expensive. It turned out later that it was the agent who was interested in betting, while the Open Champion himself was relaxed and indifferent to the idea. So I saved £50. Christopher Lee, not having touched a club for months, went out in 37. Meanwhile Weiskopf played some astonishing shots but complained of weariness. He had not been in bed for over 30 hours and his entire luggage, golf clubs excepted, had been lost en route. This subsequently got him into hot water with the management. As he had neither jacket nor tie he was promptly thrown out the moment he tried to enter the dining room. He then locked himself in his room until the manager relented. They kept up this monumental stupidity for nearly two days before peace was declared. Soon afterwards his baggage turned up anyway.

A second match was arranged. I was to play against the champion and his partner. Match eve nearly became my undoing. Breakfast was scheduled for 7 a.m. I was at a loss: what does one do before such a contest? Early to bed! was my answer. That must be the right idea, I thought. At 6.45 a.m. I received a telephone call from London. 'Are you mad?' I demanded. 'Not really,' came the reply. 'You rang me at a quarter to five this morning and said for God's sake ring you at quarter to seven.' I struggled into a cold bath and prepared to take on the Open Champion. I should, perhaps, mention that I did have a partner. His name was Peter Oosterhuis.

To my surprise, soon after 7.30 we were ushered towards the practice ground. The great man – I should now say the great men – wished to practise. Why, I wondered, but not for very long. What with the time of the morning and a persistent drizzle all about, I soon decided to join them. Before that, however, I was introduced to my secret weapon. He was about five feet one and a half inches tall, no longer young and ill-protected against the rain. He approached through the soaking wet grass. 'My name is Mr MacDonald,' he announced, 'and I am your caddy for today.'

'How splendid,' I said. 'And how are you this fine damp morning, Mr MacDonald?'

'The weather is of little consequence,' he replied, 'but one thing we must have clear: who is going to be in charge?'

'Why, you are, Mr MacDonald,' I said. 'Sir,' I added.

'Aye, that's right,' he replied. 'I'm glad you've got the right idea,' he went on as a bank of mist rolled in to join the drizzle. 'What's your handicap?'

'Fifteen, Mr MacDonald, I'm afraid.'

'Nonsense! Afraid! You and I are going out there to play fifteen handicap golf. Now come along. You must hit some balls. If the professionals need to practise I'm damned sure you do.'

The rain and mist delayed our start until after nine o'clock. In the meantime I was introduced to Peter Oosterhuis, another giant, probably even taller than the Open Champion and certainly solider. The drizzle was doing my headache a lot of good, and when hot drinks were proffered by the BBC I realised that the contest was to be televised – another unforeseen terror. I wished fervently that I was in an alehouse in London. Visibility improved by the moment, and by 9.30 hostilities got under way. No air shot was forthcoming, so that was a relief. The great men drove off into the far distant mist. After a hole or two I thought I ought to consult my partner for advice. 'What do you think I should do for this shot, Mr Oosterhuis?' I asked.

'Take your maximum weapon and hit it as hard as you can,' he

replied. There was a whisper in my ear. 'No, no, no. Take your
six-iron and poke it down there in front of yon bunker.' And by
following advice such as this from Mr MacDonald and ignoring
that of my mighty partner I found things actually going rather
well. There is, by the way, no question of being given another go
in these contests: no Mulligans or take twos. When you have
struck, or failed to strike, the ball, that's *it*. Humiliation is always
just round the corner.

The King's Course at Gleneagles is a delight, no less than the
Queen's. The turf is unique: no question of tired feet or terrible
lies in the middle of the fairway. Each fairway is private, protected
from its neighbour by grassy banks, not to mention bracken,
heather, occasional pine trees and other forgotten horrors. As the
mist disappeared the Perthshire hills and the Auchterarder distil-
lery came into view. Thus, there is no problem if you can't hit the
ball into the right place: you can enjoy the magnificent views of
the one or mentally savour the products of the other. With the
mist now faded away one could admire the shots of the Open
Champion and of my partner. They both seemed to strike it a
country mile from the tee and with astonishing accuracy from
other positions on the course.

I wondered how the Champion was feeling. He had joined in a
certain amount of revelry the night before. At dinner he was constantly questioned on the finer points, and the points tended to
become finer as the hour drew later. An umbrella was produced,
and with this improbable substitute Weiskopf gave instruction in
the fundamentals as well as in the finer points to the posse of
admirers clustered about him.

As the hour had grown even later the roles had rather tended
to be reversed, until it was the Open Champion who was on the
receiving end ('let's have a look at your grip, Tom . . . hmmm . . .
no, *I* don't hold it like that at all . . .'). The whole gamut of
technique was analysed, backswing, downswing, grip, position at
address, follow-through, with the umbrella passing from one
adviser to the next. Weiskopf remained genial throughout, and did
not decide to rebuild his swing on the strength of this abundance of
ad hoc advice. I fancied, however, that he might perhaps have a

thin headache the following morning. And back to the following morning we must go.

I don't know if there are golf courses in the United States which include heather in their armoury, and it probably doesn't matter. But it is a potent enemy. I remember a friend saying to me during a foursome at Walton Heath, 'Only two options for dealing with heather, old chap: a brassie or a niblick, and no guarantees attached to either.' On this particular day the American contingent had a desperate penchant for visiting the heather. Maybe they liked its pretty appearance and wished to admire it from closer to. But it cost them the match, by about five shots. The harsh regime of the diminutive MacDonald paid off handsomely. Fifteen handicap golf was played, and with a little help from Peter Oosterhuis the Open Champion was overcome, and that's why I feel that the adventures of an ordinary golfer can be quite fantastical.

A Good Walk Spoiled?

Mike Seabrook

I'd better come clean. I don't know much about golf. Or rather, since all writers are supposed to be, at bottom, seekers after Truth, I don't know anything about golf. It is true that my finest hour as a sportsman, in any game whatever, was a hole in one at the thirteenth at Cromer. Unfortunately it was the thirteenth at Cromer putting green, which tends to remove much of the glitter from the achievement. I remember bounding after the ball as it negotiated the sinuous contours of the 'course' (I was about thirteen, and still capable of such things) and, as I saw the ball drop, magically, into the hole, I whirled my putter aloft and brandished it triumphantly above my head. It broke one of the string of ornamental coloured light bulbs festooned all over the little green. And that, alas, is the beginning and the end of my personal experience of the game of golf.

Unfortunately the list of impediments to my ever becoming a golfer does not begin and end as briskly. Apart from being too fat to relish the exercise afforded by a round of golf, and too lazy and averse to pain to remedy that condition, I chance to have been born with a body that resolutely refuses to do what I tell it. This is an insurmountable handicap in all games: games I love, such as cricket and rugby, games I don't, such as football and tennis; and games that I might like if I could summon up the courage to try them – foremost among them golf.

My reactions are those of an elderly and tired snail. All right, you say: reactions are less important in still-ball games; and that is true. I did, indeed, become a very passable snooker-player, thanks entirely to dour and unremitting practice and that very fact that reflexes didn't matter. But co-ordination does matter – raising the club all that way in the air, and then trying to whirl it round and make contact with that piddling little ball. And if there's anything about me that's even less developed than my reflexes, it's my co-ordination. And that single small entry on the credit side of the ledger is further cancelled out by the last in the catalogue of my unfittedness: without my glasses I am so short-sighted as to be more or less blind. I can, admittedly, *see* a double-decker bus in time to avoid being run over by it. But beyond a range of about twenty yards I recognise it for the London bus it is only because intellect informs me that nothing else of that size, shape and particular shade of red is likely to be coming rapidly towards me in a London thoroughfare. If it was a matter of eyesight alone it could be, quite literally, anything.

'Well, all right,' you may be murmuring; 'but you needn't *be* without your glasses, need you? It's not rugby we're talking about.' A fair point – except for one thing. I sweat. A lot. I emphatically don't perspire. I sweat, it is fair to say, like a cart-horse; and that is in the normal way of things – it's just the way I'm made. If I engage in anything involving the slightest physical exertion, it positively cascades out of me; and the first result is that within minutes of starting a round of golf – by the time, say, I'd lugged my bag from the clubhouse to the first tee – such a drenching downpour would have transferred itself from my forehead and hair to my spectacles that they would from then on be as much use to me as they would in a 100 yards butterfly. One needs make no mention of rain.

All this makes a convincing case for my non-golfership. Added to it is the singularly unhelpful nature to the layman of golfing jargon, and an odd, but substantial reluctance on the part of TV golfing commentators to help out in this respect – resulting in my never completely understanding what is going on on a golf course. This is very strange. The golfing team are otherwise without exception models of their trade: fathomlessly knowledgeable, unrufflable, without any tendency to hysteria and, greatest gift and blessing of all for TV people, masters of the priceless art of knowing when to keep the mouth *shut*: you just don't hear Peter Alliss and his friends determinedly informing you of that which your eyes have just witnessed. Even cricket commentators are only too ready to tell you that ''e's 'it that very 'ard, an it's knocked the umpire's 'at off . . .' and so on. At the other end of the scale, only Dan Maskell dares to assume that if we are watching the tennis on TV we must be able to see, and tells us therefore not what the player has just done, but why he did it.

The golf chaps are somewhere in between – though mercifully closer to Maskell's perfection than to the only-too-evident mortality of the rest. Their own special vice is to speak fluently, affably and evidently appositely about 'borrow', and 'shanking', and even, from time to time, about 'Greensome Stablefords' and 'four-ball foursomes'. Their airy assumption that we all know all about such mysteries may be meant as a compliment; in my case all it succeeds in doing is to leave me frustrated and mystified; rather as if someone were to read a sentence in a foreign language in which he knew every word except the one absolutely crucial one: we know *something* sat on the mat; but if the word 'cat' is the one we don't know, the sentence could mean, almost literally, anything. Elephant? Armchair? Little green man with three heads? Bogey?

I have, admittedly, worked out some of the jargon for myself: I know about birdies, eagles and, though I've never seen one, albatrosses. But I wish perennially that someone would tell me (a) why golfers only wear one glove and (b) why no commentator in the history of the game has ever been heard to explain why.

So far we've had a convincing catalogue of reasons why I have never played golf, probably never will, and wouldn't be any good at it if I did, and a minor gripe about the generally superlative TV commentary. It leaves me with two questions to answer if I can. Why, given all these handicaps, do I find the game so irresistibly fascinating and, in particular, so irresistibly *funny*?

The two questions are inextricably linked, I believe. As a keen student of human nature I am anxious to find out exactly why a game so self-evidently absurd holds me so mercilessly in its thrall; and as someone who concluded in adolescence that the only hope of remaining sane was to laugh at mankind's antics on this earth

at all times if possible I take the view that it is the very absurdity of the game that makes the first question so endlessly interesting. If golf was something stupendously serious and important – like, say, the economy – it would be desperately uninteresting; like, say, the economy.

I even find the name of the game funny. Golf. Golf golf golf. Or goff. If you are upper class you don't play golf, just as you don't look in the mirror over the mantelpiece. No, you adjust your cap in the glass above the chimney-piece, and then you go orf to play goff. Probably with someone called Rafe.

Professor Tolkien is alone, I believe, in claiming to have discovered the origin of the name, and his account reveals clearly that he, too, found the word funny. In *The Hobbit*, he tells of a great battle, fought when the earth was young, between goblins and hobbits. A great hobbit of old 'charged the ranks of the goblins of Mount Gram in the Battle of the Green Fields, and knocked their king Golfimbul's head clean off with a wooden club. It sailed a hundred yards through the air and went down a rabbit hole, and in this way the battle was won and the game of Golf invented at the same moment.' It sounds as likely as any other theory to me.

So what *is* the appeal of the game? And why does it arouse such fierce passions, among its devotees and its detractors alike? I can't remember ever meeting a golfer who was *just* a golfer, merely that and nothing more. They have been, to a man (and woman) golf *fanatics*. I like that: whatsoever thy hand findeth to do, do it with thy might. If a thing's worth doing at all, it's worth hurling yourself at it like a bull at a gate. The story of the man who evoked his opponent's amazed admiration by standing in silence while a funeral cortège passed on a nearby road, thus destroying his concentration and losing the game, and said when the opponent asked why he had done so, 'Well, we *had* been married for thirty years,' is not so very far from the truth, if the golfers I have known are anything to go by. And people who don't like golf tend, I find, not just to dislike it, but to *hate* it, with a ferocity of loathing that is difficult to understand until one discovers – and one almost always *does* discover – that the person at some time expended vast quantities of money, effort, profanity and sweat on trying to play the game, and failed.

Let us, however, get one thing straight from the start. Mark Twain was quite wrong to call a round of golf a good walk spoiled. Walking, in itself, is the most boring, pointless and, since the merciful invention of wheeled transport, *unnecessary* activity known to man. If it is to be done at all it *needs* a purpose, of some kind, to justify it; and beating the hell out of someone at golf is as good a purpose as any. (Bird-watching, fossil collecting or annoying farmers by maliciously walking once a year along footpaths they would like to close are equally valid purposes, but that's by the way.)

I'm sure that much of the appeal of the game – especially, perhaps only, to armchair golfers such as myself – is that it puts people into silly postures: Bernhard Langer up a tree, that American up to his knees in lake, people with one foot down a rabbit hole and the other about three feet higher up a bank, in a bed of nettles, and so on. This is especially satisfying when it's the professionals one is watching thus made to look silly. Golf has a wonderful way of reducing the colossally paid to the status of ordinary, fallible human beings, prone to the vagaries of fortune, wind and weather like everybody else, unparalleled in any other game. It appeals to the secret communist, the demonic, dog-in-the-manger, downward-levelling little *schadenfreude*-artist that lurks somewhere in the deeps of every soul.

A footballer, a rugby player, an automaton in the mechanised certainties of modern basketball, even a cricketer, except when he is batting, can hide to a certain merciful extent. A golfer, never. I suppose it is possible, in the darkest pleasures of the imagination, to conceive of other sporting activities producing the same kind of pleasure: I mean, it would be wonderful to watch an entire synchronised swimming team drowning at the same moment, preferably at the Olympics (swimming, once the ability has been acquired for the purposes of saving one's life, being the only activity known to man that is even more boring, pointless and unnecessary than walking). But golf humbles its devotees, even the most talented of them, regularly. That Hamlet Cigars ad in the bunker, where we see only the head of the club alternating with little puffs of sand, gets very close to the heart of the game's essentially farcical nature.

All this being the case, I particularly like the fact that among all professional games-players the golfers are almost alone in remaining equable, courteous, fair and good-tempered, magnanimous in victory and pretty fatalistic and cheerful in defeat. On the other hand, I enjoy equally the fervour and desperation that the game, in an odd paradox, seems able to inspire in even the mildest-mannered of its *amateur* devotees – the clubs snapped over the knee (a tougher proposition now, I should imagine, with carbon fibre and tungsten steel, or titanium alloy, or whatever they're making clubs of these days), the balls hurled into lakes (and, on occasion, at opponents, I've been told), the rages, tantrums and solemn oaths before witnesses never to lay a hand on a club again.

Golf is among the very rare sporting activities that make genuinely good theatre – or, at any rate, good cinema. The golf game in *Goldfinger* is one of the few sporting scenes in cinema history that I know of that has really worked – though I wonder if it would have done had it been anyone other than Sean Connery playing the scene. The game does have the potential for high drama – probably because of the very strong emphasis it puts on the talent, temperament, fortune and way of greeting fortune of the individual. Its one-on-one nature gives it automatic, built-in dramatic tension. Team games have got drama – a rugby match, still more a cricket match, can be positively electrifying; but they do it in different ways, involving excitement, bitten nails, inability to watch at vital stages, and so on. But much, indeed most, of this tension is linked to a fixed period of play and the agonising wait for the final whistle or the last over. With these games, it is all climax. With golf, the drama may be quieter, but it's continuous.

Then, the golfer's enemies are less predictable than those of the footballer or cricketer. Of course every player of every game can make a fool of himself at any moment, and all games are to some extent at the mercy of the weather. But in most games they are background matters. The teams realise they've got to play their rugby in a howling gale, so they make the necessary adjustments to the theory by which they propose to play the game, and then try to implement it. The cricketers know they will have to take the wind, or humidity or whatever, into account, and they do so. The real enemy is, still, the opposition.

In golf, by contrast, the opponent may be little more than a sparring partner, even a pacemaker. The weather is a potentially deadly enemy at every individual stroke – and an enemy in a different guise each time. The slightest variation in the conditions can turn an almost identical lie into a totally different problem to be solved. And the fact that there is far more time to stand and think about it than in, say, rugby or cricket, makes it worse rather than better: if a problem arises in a rugby match, say, there is very little time for the patient to stand there agonising about it. With several tons of broken-nosed thug bearing down on him at appalling velocity and with malice only too evidently aforethought, there is great virtue in saying to oneself, 'Oh well, this looks the most likely way out of this hole, and I'd better take it while the going's good.' In other words, shit or bust. There is no such healthy deterrent to rational thought in golf.

The lie of the land itself is an equally deadly enemy, changing its shape like an amoeba between strokes. But the greatest enemy of the lot, in golf, it seems to me, watching enthralled from my armchair, is none of these. The real enemy is the player himself. Every action he makes is a potential disaster waiting to happen. The weather and the lie he cannot help. His method of countering them, he can. It's all down to him. In this sense, it seems to me that golf is an even higher form of self-immolation than snooker. In snooker there is no weather, and no lie of the land. There is the lie of the balls, but that is within the power of the player to make favourable or not. Golf is the only game that pits the player against an opponent, the weather, the minutest details of a large chunk of local topography and his own nervous system, all at the same time.

It's also the only game that does all this to the player several times, over a period as long as a week or even longer – a point which might be borne in mind by Americans before they make that unkind quip they're fond of about Test cricket being the only game that can take five days and still not produce a result. In a golf tournament you can go out and walk what looks like several thousand miles, suffer death by flaying alive trying to hit the beastly ball out of a gorse bush, eat a small dustbin of valium to keep the nervous system in check, and still end up, a week later, not making the cut. This is a game that Cromwell would have approved of, and probably Zeno of Citium and St Augustine as well.

But every purgatorio has its paradiso, and golf finds solace in a well-established tradition of the 19th hole. This adds a wholly necessary element of humanity to the proceedings. As a former rugby player and a still active cricketer, I have always averred, without being open to argument on the matter, that no form of games activity is complete without its due and proper element of associated drinking activity. If you couldn't drink after rugby I'd have had nothing to do with the game; and the same goes still more for cricket: it is, quite simply, inseparable from the drinking of beer or cider. Now golfers seem to me to tend towards a distressingly lean and hungry look. But this can't be a true representation of them as a breed. The stories of the nineteenth are simply too abundant to be false; and they all *sound* true, too. I conclude that golfers simply sweat all the drinks out of their systems as they trek their way round their five-mile game. And since, as I observed a while back, there are no mere golfers, only fanatical golfers, I conclude further that there's always another round to play, after the celebrations in the clubhouse. This is the only explanation I can think of for this dismaying tendency of golfers to look fit and lean.

The professionals, of course, I except from the last observations. It seems to me that these days the life of any professional games player is such an atrociously miserable-gutted and earnest affair that no sane and properly balanced man would contemplate taking it up for one moment. Imagine becoming a professional cricketer, for instance, and then having to go for training runs, and even circuit training and iron-pumping! On second thoughts, recoil in appalled horror from imagining any such thing, and pour an extra large freshener into your glass. And the professional golfers tend to look even fitter than our cricketers have come to look. And they don't seem to get many more laughs out of their game, either. One presumes therefore that they, too, put themselves through the same kind of dismal, soul-destroying, personality-crushing rituals in the cause of bodily stamina. One can only pity them, since there is no way in which I, at any rate, can imagine the tide of this obsession with training being turned back.

Another way in which golfers in general (once again the professionals appear to be the exceptions) seem to be a happier breed than many sportsmen is that their stories are the best sporting stories, by far. There are countless cricket stories, but they have a tendency to misty-eyed nostalgia for sunny days and glorious players of days gone by. Rugby has its rude songs, and no doubt other games have their tales. But there is no doubt in my mind that golf *stories*, generally, are the best of all.

They are often marked by their wit and subtlety, too. Jimmy Tarbuck, not a comedian one would automatically associate with subtlety, tells of a threesome who, on driving off from the first tee, each show the others the make of golf ball they're using, as, I gather, is necessary. The first two show a Penfold hearts and a Dunlop and drive off without comment. Then the third holds out his ball and announces 'Bleeper No. 1'. The other two look up in surprise. 'Bleeper?' they say. 'Never heard of that one.'

'It's great,' he says, showing them. 'It's got a light sensor inside. If you land in heavy rough or bushes, the sensor detects the reduced light, and sets off a tiny bleeping device inside the ball. So all you have to do is follow the sound, and you can't lose your ball.'

'And that's not all,' he goes on as they make admiring noises. 'It's got a fog detector, too. So if you land in a patch of mist, it sets off the bleeper, and at the same time a panel in the casing slides back – it's too well-made to be visible now – and a tiny iodine quartz light flashes, so you can find your way to it.' They admire it further. 'It's got a water sensor, too,' he says proudly. 'If you land in water, it senses it, and as well as the bleeper, it lets out four little rubber floats, and a tiny motor inside sets it moving until it senses that it's reached dry land. You simply can't get yourself lost.'

'That's wonderful,' the other two chorus enviously. 'Wherever did you get it?'

'I found it,' he says.

Another, allegedly true, concerns a hard old professional propping up the bar in the clubhouse when a member comes tottering in, trembling all over and yelping for brandy. When he has swallowed three doubles in as many seconds the old pro asks him what's troubling him. After another restorative the man calms down enough to tell the story. 'I mis-hit off the fifth tee,' he says, 'and my ball flew out across the main road and hit a man on a bike. He went all over the road, a petrol tanker swerved to avoid him, crashed into a pub, caught fire and eventually exploded. There's people hurt, thousands of pounds of damage, and it's all because I couldn't hit the ball straight,' he wails, frantic with remorse. 'What in the world am I to do?'

'Try keeping the thumb of your bottom hand a bit further round to the right when you address the ball,' says the old pro, turning back to his drinking companion. 'As I was saying . . .'

Nearly all the golf stories I've heard have had this strong element of wit, depreciatory of golfers or of the game itself, about them, and I think it's a very attractive trait. A game that its devotees take so deadly seriously, which can yet inspire such a depth of wit at its own expense is evidently a game worth taking an interest in. Golf is a terrible, hopeless addiction, it seems: it makes its devotees willing to trudge miles in any manner of weather, lugging a huge, incommodious and appallingly heavy bag with them, in pursuit of a tiny and fantastically expensive ball, in a fanatical attempt to direct it into a hole the size of a beer glass half a mile away. If anything could be better calculated to convince one of the essential lunacy of the human race, I haven't found it. And yet it gives one a breath of hope when one perceives that its most ardent devotees are, somewhere very deep inside, fully aware of the absurdity of their consuming passion. It is probably impossible to derive enjoyment from this life at all unless you are a little insane, at least. But it is well to be aware of the fact.

To adapt George Santayana, golf is essentially useless, as life is; but both lend utility to their conditions. He was talking about music, but it applies as well to golf, which is why I shall still be awake in the middle of the night after writing this, utterly unable to switch off my television until an obscure satellite station, with commentary in something that might be Walloon or Finnish but could equally well be Serbo-Croat or Double-Dutch, ends its transmission of the third day of the Ouagadougou Open.

Notes on the Contributors

Peter Alliss

Britain's Mr Golf, Peter Alliss, became a professional golfer at 15. Thereafter he played in the Ryder Cup eight times and the Canada Cup (now the World Cup) ten times, meanwhile winning 21 major individual events. Since retirement he has written numerous books on the game and worked as a golf course architect; but there is no doubt that he is best known for his unique style of television commentary on golf: unflappable, knowledgeable, soft-spoken, witty and urbane, and blessed with the gift of knowing when to let the pictures do the talking.

Richard Condon

Born in New York, Richard Condon is one of the most versatile novelists currently writing in the United States. His many novels have been translated into many languages and several have been turned into films, notably *The Manchurian Candidate*, the book for which he is probably best known. He has lived in Paris, Madrid, Geneva, Mexico City, New York, and, now, Texas.

Sir Michael Davies

Recently retired as a judge of the High Court, Sir Michael Davies is a bencher of Lincoln's Inn. As Mr Justice Michael Davies he carried on the tradition of judicial wit, being best known perhaps for his recommendation to the jury in a libel case just before he retired that damages should not be colossal but perhaps equivalent to the value of his own car, 'a clapped-out Volvo'. As a result of the publicity this attracted he subsequently apologised to his car in open court, announcing that he had promised it a full service and wax-polish in damages. He lives with his wife in London and Worcestershire.

BILL DEEDES

Former Conservative Member of Parliament for Ashford in Kent, where he still lives, Bill Deedes is also a former editor of the *Daily Telegraph*. Now Lord Deedes, he still writes a lively current affairs column and is known as the famous Bill of the 'Dear Bill' letters in *Private Eye*, and as a lifelong cricket and golf aficionado, bon viveur and old-fashioned English gentleman.

JOHN EBDON

Formerly Director of the London Planetarium, John Ebdon was for many years also one of those versatile broadcasters of the old-style BBC who could talk about almost any subject under the sun for twenty minutes and make it compulsive listening. He lives in Wembley, but hopes to translate himself and his wife to the sun of the Greek Islands.

BRIAN GLANVILLE

Educated at Charterhouse, Brian Glanville has written both novels and non-fiction. He has also achieved the remarkable distinction of writing literately on football, which he has been doing for the *Sunday Times* without a break since 1958. Keenly interested in all sports, he plays football for Chelsea Casuals. He lives in west London.

DAME JOAN HAMMOND

Dame Joan Hammond's illustrious career as a singer of opera, oratorio and Lieder began in her native Australia and took her to triumphs in every major opera house and concert hall in the world. Less well-known are the facts that she was a volunteer ambulance driver in London during the Blitz, and that she was a champion golfer, winning the New South Wales Ladies State title three times and once finishing runner-up in the Australian Open. In a golfing tournament between the contributors to this anthology (what a nice thought) she would almost certainly play one of the editors in the Final.

GEORGE V. HIGGINS

George V. Higgins graduated in English and worked as a reporter before getting a law degree and working in the Massachusetts Attorney-General's office. His experiences in the Organised Crime Section and the Criminal Division there are drawn on for his tough-talk crime thrillers, which have achieved cult status on both sides of the Atlantic. He was recently appointed a Professor at his old *alma mater*, Boston University. He lives in Massachusetts.

MARTIN JOHNSON

Martin Johnson was a surprising and inspired choice as the cricket correspondent of the *Independent* when it was founded in 1986: surprising because he was recruited not from one of the existing national papers but from a provincial paper, the Leicester *Mercury*, and inspired because he has since been consistently the funniest sports reporter in 'Fleet Street'. Those who eagerly await and devour his cricket reports are known to include many who have not the slightest interest in cricket. He lives in Leicestershire.

JEREMY KEMP

Jeremy Kemp has been one of Britain's leading screen actors for over thirty years. He served his apprenticeship on the stage but attained immediate stardom as one of the original four policemen in the long-running classic 'Z-Cars' TV series. After starring in another TV classic, 'Colditz', he has appeared – often above the title – in over thirty feature films, including *Darling Lili* with Julie Andrews and the late Rock Hudson, and half a dozen mini-series, including the blockbusters 'Peter the Great' and Herman Wouk's 'Winds of War'.

Miles Kington

A former editor of the late and lamented *Punch*, Miles Kington has written columns for over twenty years, humorous, witty and just occasionally serious and astonishingly savage, for *The Times* and, since 1986, the *Independent*. He is clearly the spiritual heir and successor to J. B. Morton, the legendary 'Beachcomber' of the *Daily Express*. He is also a railway buff and played double bass for the music group Instant Sunshine. He lives near Bath.

Frank Muir

One of Britain's best-loved humourists, Frank Muir was for 17 years half of one of the all-time great comedy script-writing partnerships, with Denis Norden. He has been a regular panellist on such TV shows as 'My Word', 'Call my Bluff' and, still, 'My Music', has received numerous awards for his work in light entertainment and broadcasting, has written many books, from the flippant to the scholarly, and has garnered a CBE and two honorary doctorates of letters from British universities.

Edward Pearce

Edward Pearce has written the Parliamentary sketch column for the *Daily Telegraph*, a current affairs column for the *Sunday Times*, was briefly *Cross-Bencher* in the *Sunday Express*, and now writes a pungent column for the *Guardian*. He also writes for periodicals as diverse as the *New Statesman*, *Marxism Today* and the journal of the Police Federation. He is a passionate lover of classical music, and reviews regularly for a hi-fi magazine. Known and adored by many for having possibly the most ferocious turn of phrase in 'Fleet Street', he was kicked out of the sketch spot on the *Telegraph* for using it on Margaret Thatcher. He has written four books of hilarious and devastating contemporary political comment, a biography of John Major, and an on-the-stump diary of the 1992 General Election. He lives in Buckinghamshire.

Chris Plumridge

Chris Plumridge is the golf columnist for the *Sunday Telegraph*, where his lyrical prose style is widely admired. He has been writing about the game for twenty-five years, and playing it for forty, for much of that time off a handicap of 3, which makes him a very likely finalist in an imaginary tournament for our contributors. He has written eight books on golf, and contributed to many newspapers and periodicals about the game. He lives in the next village to Edward Pearce in Buckinghamshire.

SIMON RAVEN

Simon Raven is one of Britain's finest living novelists and belletrists. His ten-novel sequence *Alms for Oblivion* savaged the English upper and middle classes as they had never been savaged before, and he has recently completed a new cycle of seven novels in which he continued the process. His volumes of belles-lettres are a mixture of autobiography and mordant diagnosis of the state of the nation over the past few decades. He has also written plays and radio and TV scripts, among the most celebrated being *The Pallisers* and *Edward and Mrs Simpson*. He lives in Kent.

MIKE SEABROOK

After a classical education which he wishes had gone on longer, Mike Seabrook ran away to be a policeman, serving in London for some years. Subsequently, after years of Byronic gloom as an advertising copywriter and technical author he ran away again, this time to be a full-time author. He has published three novels, two collections of cricket essays and the only wholly truthful book ever written by an insider about the British police, and writes a regular column in the *New Law Journal*. He lives with his wife beside a lake in the Jura mountains of eastern France.

DONALD SOPER

The Rev. Donald Soper, since 1965 Baron Soper, has been for many years a prominent and, many would say, turbulent luminary of the Methodist Church. He was President of the West London Mission from 1936 to 1978, and has been associated with various quasi-political causes, including the League Against Cruel Sports.

He has written widely on his faith and the difficulties it poses for its adherents, and is known as an outspoken and fearless thinker.

BILL TIDY

One of Britain's best-known cartoonists, Bill Tidy's unmistakable style has been seen in virtually every publication in Britain that prints cartoons, from *Punch* to *Private Eye* and even a computer trade magazine. He is also a playwright, writer and regular broadcaster on radio and television. He lives in Derbyshire.

DONALD TRELFORD

Donald Trelford is the longest-standing editor of any British national newspaper, having edited *The Observer* since 1975. He spent many years working for newspapers in Africa, has won numerous awards for his work in journalism and served on many committees in journalism, broadcasting and public affairs. He is an unusual combination of high-intellectual editor of a heavyweight paper and all-round sports enthusiast. His books include a passionate, literate and very funny one on snooker.

JOHN UPDIKE

By general consent one of the two or three finest stylists writing in English today, John Updike was born in Pennsylvania, educated at Harvard and began his writing career as a journalist on *The New Yorker*. Among his many novels the 'Rabbit' tetralogy are perhaps his best known and loved, demonstrating his perception, clear-eyed and free from illusion but always merciful, of the faults of the ordinary American. He is also a master of the most rarefied and threatened of literary forms, the short story.

IAN WALLACE

In a long career as an opera singer, Ian Wallace sang most of the great baritone roles, especially at Glyndebourne. He is also a much-loved broadcaster, being a long-standing regular panellist on 'My Music' on radio and TV. He has recorded the complete Gilbert and Sullivan light operas with Sir Malcolm Sargent, sung the comic songs of Flanders and Swann, and acted in the award-winning TV adaptation of Tom Sharpe's *Porterhouse Blue*.

JOSEPH WAMBAUGH

One of the handful of truly great novelists currently writing in English, Joseph Wambaugh is assuredly *the* greatest chronicler of the American police, which he writes about with total and uncompromising accuracy – not surprisingly, for he served in the Los Angeles PD for fourteen years. He also treats the police as a microcosm and an image of contemporary American society as a whole, and issues his verdict in a series of ferocious black tragi-comedies in which pity is always close to the surface, but always at risk of being burned away by the savagery, neurosis and danger of the modern urban jungle. He has interspersed his novels with occasional works of non-fiction, including one on the Leicester sex murders and the first use of DNA-matching.